PRAISE FOR ROCKET FUEL

"*Rocket Fuel* is a powerful model for freeing up entrepreneurial Visionaries to do what they do best. It fills a void that undermines most entrepreneurial companies. Gino and Mark provide a practical game plan for building an organization that perfectly combines vision and integration."

—*Dan Sullivan*
President and Founder, Strategic Coach®

"Contrary to popular belief, it takes not one but two entrepreneurs to build a great company, and they have dramatically different roles. In this brilliant book, Gino Wickman and Mark C. Winters explain the vital importance of having both a Visionary and an Integrator—and show how that relationship can provide the 'rocket fuel' your company needs to achieve its full potential."

—*Bo Burlingham*
Editor-at-Large, Inc. *magazine, and author of* Small Giants *and* Finish Big: How Great Entrepreneurs Exit Their Companies on Top

THE TRACTION LIBRARY

WANT EVEN BETTER RESULTS AND MORE BUSINESS SUCCESS?

Every person on your team must be equipped with the right information and tools to implement EOS, the Entrepreneurial Operating System® purely throughout your organization. With The Traction Library, your entire company—from leadership to management to employees—will understand their role and be better equipped to help your company succeed.

HERE'S HOW!

AVAILABLE BOOKS	WHO IT'S FOR
Traction	For everyone
Rocket Fuel	For the Visionary and the Integrator
Get a Grip (*Traction*'s fable)	For the leadership team
How to Be a Great Boss	For leaders, managers, and supervisors
What the Heck is EOS?	For all employees, managers, and supervisors

Visit **www.eosworldwide.com** to get everything you need to fully implement EOS in your company today.

ROCKET FUEL

THE ONE ESSENTIAL COMBINATION THAT WILL GET YOU MORE OF WHAT YOU WANT FROM YOUR BUSINESS

GINO WICKMAN
AND MARK C. WINTERS

BenBella Books, Inc.
Dallas, TX

BenBella

BenBella Books, Inc.
10440 N. Central Expressway
Suite #800
Dallas, TX 75231
www.benbellabooks.com
Send feedback to feedback@benbellabooks.com

Printed in the United States of America
10 9 8 7 6 5

ISBN-13: 978-1-942952-31-2 (paperback)

The Library of Congress has cataloged the hardcover edition as follows:
Wickman, Gino.
    Rocket fuel: the one essential combination that will get you more of what you want from your business / Gino Wickman, Mark C. Winters.
        pages   cm
    Includes bibliographical references and index.
        ISBN 978-1-941631-15-7 (hardback) — ISBN 978-1-941631-16-4 (electronic)   1. Success in business.   2. Creative ability in business.   3. Small business—Management.   I. Winters, Mark C.   II. Title.
    HF5386.W49427 2015
    658.4'09—dc23
                                                                    2014041349

Editing by Heather Butterfield
Copyediting by Stacia Seaman
Proofreading by Greg Teague, Clarissa
    Phillips, Brittney Martinez, and
    Cameron Proffitt
Cover design by Faceout Studio

Text design and composition by
    Publishers' Design and Production
    Services, Inc.
Graphic design by Drew Robinson
    Spork Design
Printed by Lake Book Manufacturing

Distributed to the trade by Two Rivers Distribution, an Ingram brand
www.tworiversdistribution.com

To the entrepreneur:
The 3% that creates 66% of the jobs. This book
should help you create a few more.

—Gino Wickman

To Dad, R.L. Winters, MD:
The hands of a healer, a heart for the Lord, and the
adventurous spirit of an entrepreneur . . . You've
taught me so much. I marvel at the number of lives
you've impacted—none more than mine.

And also to my beautiful wife, Beth, and my sons,
Austin, Blake, and Carson:
Everything is better when I'm with you. You are my
world. I love you beyond words.

—Mark C. Winters

CONTENTS

VISIONARY—vi·sion·ary, *noun* \ˈvi-zhə-ˌner-ē\,
First Known Use: 1702

: one who has clear ideas about what should happen
or be done in the future
: one who has a powerful imagination
: one who sees visions
: one who has unusual foresight

Dreamer, Seer, Creator

INTEGRATOR—in·te·gra·tor, *noun* \in-tə,-grā-tər\,
First Known Use: 1876

: one who integrates
: one who harmoniously unites the major functions
of a business
: one who keeps the trains running on time
: one who creates focus, accountability, and
alignment

Right Hand, Number Two, Steady Force

THE DISCOVERY

This book is a how-to manual for understanding and managing the relationship between a "Visionary" and an "Integrator." It will help you crystallize the meanings of these two roles and take your company to the next level. You will learn to utilize this partnership the right way to free yourself up, maximize your potential, and achieve everything you want from your business.

AS A VISIONARY

This is the right book for you if:

- You are an owner, founder, co-founder, or partner in a small business and you are feeling stuck, frustrated, overwhelmed, or out of control.
- You want a great second-in-command to free you up to go to the next level.

- You are not sure about looking for a president, general manager, or COO.
- You want to maximize the existing relationship with your Integrator.

AS AN INTEGRATOR

This is the right book for you if:

- You have all of the characteristics of a strong second-in-command and want to put those skills to use.
- You are sitting in the #2 seat in an organization and want to help take it to the next level.
- You are a partner to a "Visionary" type, and the relationship is strained, frustrated, or just not working right.

The message in this book is based on a discovery Gino made over 20 years ago. He applied it to a family business that he co-owned and ran for more than eight years before successfully selling the company. He has personally researched, taught, and validated this concept, working hands-on with over 125 companies and applying it directly through more than 1,500 full-day sessions with owners and leadership teams. It has been further validated by a team of dedicated EOS Implementers working with thousands of companies and by business owners in more than 10,000 companies who have read and applied the concepts outlined in two other books he has written.

It is important to note that the companies we typically work with generate revenues of $2–$50 million and range in size from 10 to 250 people. While this discovery also works with companies both larger and smaller than that range, this is our target market where these principles have been mainly validated.

What is the discovery Gino made? There are two distinct types of leaders in all small businesses: the "Visionary" and the "Integrator." One sees the future, and the other makes it happen. These two roles could not be more different from each other. That is why it is magic when they work well together. Famous examples include the combination of Walt and Roy Disney at Disney, Henry Ford and James Couzens at Ford, and Ray Kroc and Fred Turner at McDonald's. While you may think of these as large companies, they were small once. We point them out since they illustrate how vital the V/I (Visionary/Integrator) combination was in their early growth.

This book is also filled with other examples of the hundreds of thousands of unheralded small companies. While the scale is different, the two roles are still vital in building a great company. You'll learn about real world V/I examples like Joel Pearlman and Rob Dube of imageOne ($15 million in revenue), Randy Pruitt and David Bitel of Detroit Radiator ($20 million), and John Pollock and Paul Boyd of Financial Gravity ($2 million).

This discovery came about as a result of three overlapping events. They occurred in rapid succession after Gino took over running his family's business. It was in dire need of a turnaround, and he had to act fast.

The first presented itself while he was meeting with his amazing business mentor, Sam Cupp. Sam told Gino about the type of person he called a Visionary.

The second became apparent after working closely with his dad in those first six months. Gino realized his dad was the textbook definition of a Visionary and exhibited every trait you will learn about in this book.

The third he learned from Michael E. Gerber, author of the classic book *The E-Myth Revisited: Why Most Small Businesses Don't Work and What to Do About It*. Gerber used the term "integrator" in a recorded workshop to define what the person at the helm of an organization does with all of its major functions.

Combining these three created a context that made sense of the troubles Gino was facing. He realized that he was an Integrator, his dad was a Visionary, and bringing together their distinct God-given abilities could be magic—if utilized correctly. However, at the time, things were chaotic. Their intentions were good, but they were working at cross-purposes as they tried to save the company.

With this clarity, Gino immediately called a meeting of the three partners where he explained the new principles. By the end of the meeting, they achieved clarity on their roles going forward. They identified his dad as the Visionary and Gino as the Integrator (their third partner assumed the role of Sales Manager). They crystallized their roles and responsibilities and went into execution mode. It worked! They quickly turned the company around. After seven years of running it in their Visionary and Integrator roles, they returned it to growth, profitability, and sustainability. And then they successfully sold it.

Since that experience, Gino has devoted all of his working time to helping people get what they want from their businesses. The V/I dynamic is a big part of what he teaches. And to quote Danielle Kennedy, a Hall of Fame speaker with the National Speakers Association, "We teach what *we* needed the most." This passion has continued to grow. At EOS Worldwide, we now have a team of world-class EOS Implementers working with thousands of leaders and organizations to help them achieve the results they want from their businesses.

That brings in Gino's co-author. Mark C. Winters is one of our best EOS Implementers, with 20+ incredible years of his own entrepreneurial ventures and collaborations with other business owners. Gino feels blessed to have Mark join forces with him on this important work.

"Rocket Fuel," the title of this book, actually came from one of Mark's clients. In a client session that he led while we were still working on the manuscript, the client casually asked Mark, "So, what's the title going to be for your book?" Mark shared the working title, and his Visionary client responded without hesitation, "That's not the title . . . the title is *ROCKET FUEL!*"

Mark patiently said, "Okay, tell me more." The client went on to explain that while bringing on his own Integrator, they were leveraging a program to review individual profiles and interaction combinations for every role in their organization. When their expert reviewed the profile patterns for this Visionary and his new Integrator, he paused to absorb the pattern. After a brief moment, he blurted, "WOW! You guys are perfect together—you're like ROCKET FUEL!" He was right—giving birth to the title of this book. Mark has seen firsthand how their joining forces has played a big part in taking their company to the next level.

Before we begin, it is important to understand that this discovery has at its core a philosophical belief. All human beings have a God-given set of capabilities—what Dan Sullivan would call "Unique Ability®*." Or in other words, a true skill-set or genetic makeup. The premise is that all people have one. A Visionary is meant to be a Visionary, and an Integrator is meant to be an Integrator. You are either one or the other, rarely both. One University of California professor asserts the need for both an entrepreneur and a manager at the top of a company. An entrepreneur's lust needs to be counterbalanced with a manager's prudence and discipline. He is making the same point that we do with the V/I relationship, simply using different terminology. When it's structured correctly, the dynamic that exists between these two distinct leadership gifts can be magical.

We will cover everything including what the relationship should look like, how to find each other, how to work together most effectively, and how to maximize and constantly improve the relationship.

---

* The Strategic Coach and Unique Ability® are trademarks and integral concepts owned by The Strategic Coach, Inc. Unique Ability® and its derivative works are copyrights owned by The Strategic Coach, Inc. All rights reserved. Used with written permission. www.strategiccoach.com.

The road ahead will not only help you crystallize how to find, form, and manage the relationship between a Visionary and Integrator, it will help you solve the tension and frustration that inevitably accompany this dynamic relationship of two people who are wired so differently from each other.

We invite you on this journey to discover which one you are—and free yourself to embrace it. That is our ultimate message. Figure out which one you are, assume that role, and excel!

We take great pride in sharing this message with you. We have the privilege of spending every day teaching business leaders. We witness the beneficial results achieved by defining and clarifying these two vital roles. With them, companies gain faster growth, more peace of mind, more freedom, higher profitability, more fun, and considerably increased cohesiveness. We have the great fortune to help liberate Visionaries from the shackles of the day-to-day details. We unleash their creativity to grow their organizations and capitalize on industry trends. Integrators find validation of their unique talent, grabbing the reins of a company day-to-day and creating organizational clarity, accountability, focus, and harmony.

What we are about to share is a science. It's real. It's powerful. When harnessed, it is very effective. It may be your way to finally break through the ceiling that's been hanging over you for so long.

PART ONE

THE CONTEXT

CHAPTER 1

THE VISIONARY

A re you a Visionary? Has anyone ever called you that? Maybe they see something in you that you don't fully recognize about yourself—at least not yet. Or perhaps it's something you've always known.

If you are a Visionary, you are one of only 3% of the population that create two-thirds of the new jobs in our economy. (This figure comes from John F. Dini, in his book *Hunting in a Farmers World: Celebrating the Mind of an Entrepreneur.*)

The concept of the Visionary within an organization is one of the great breakthroughs experienced by our clients. We've even had them go on to teach this concept to MBA students at universities on our behalf. Understanding and implementing this concept is both eye-opening and empowering. Frankly, it has also kept some partners from killing each other. Let's explore what life looks like for a Visionary.

HERE'S WHAT VISIONARIES BRING TO AN ORGANIZATION

To start, you should realize that the following characteristics are typical attributes. No Visionary has 100% of them. A good rule of thumb is that if you match up on 80% of the traits outlined in this section, you are a Visionary.

As a Visionary you are extremely passionate about your product, service, company, and customers. When you look up "passion" in the dictionary, your picture is there. You are very entrepreneurial, a creator, and likely a founder of your firm. Most often we see *external* titles like Owner, Founder, CEO, Chairman, or President on your business card. Yet we strongly believe that *internally* referring to roles more by what people do (e.g., Visionary or Integrator) creates clarity and does a much better job than traditional corporate titles of capturing the true contribution of each person within an organization.

The Idea Generator. As a Visionary, you have lots of ideas. You typically have ten new ideas a week. Many of them may not be so good, or at least not a fit with the company's primary focus. Some may even be dangerous. However, a few are absolutely brilliant. And those few great ideas keep the organization growing. Those great ideas can take companies to the moon. For this reason, you are invaluable.

Rob Dube, the Integrator and co-owner of imageOne, a $15 million company providing managed print services and workflow solutions, reflects on his partner and Visionary Joel Pearlman's history. Joel's "big idea" of joining a purchasing group led to considerably better margins and product knowledge. He then advocated selling the company and later buying it back. His vision to define the company's 10-year target of $60 million in revenue and $6 million in profit inspired the entire company. (Incidentally, they are on track to hit that target.) In addition, he found and closed a huge customer that represents 10% of total company revenue. Rob says, "I certainly have had to filter a lot of Joel's ideas, but none of these things would have happened if Joel were not here."

As a Visionary, you are very creative. You're great at devising solutions to big problems, not the little practical ones. You are a learner. You enjoy discovering new ideas, learning about them, and figuring out how they can work for the company. When you hit a roadblock, you study to find the answers. You teach visually, drawing diagrams on whiteboards, flip charts, yellow legal pads, napkins, or whatever happens to be within reach. A key value you bring as a Visionary is this ability to discover and figure out new ways to make things work.

"Innovators [Visionaries] find, in their lives and work, something disharmonious that common sense overlooks or denies." This quote comes from the book *The Innovator's Way*, where authors Denning and Dunham reference the book *Disclosing New Worlds* to describe this first step Visionaries take in the process of innovation.

The Big Picture. You are fantastic with important clients, vendors, suppliers, and financial relationships—the big external relationships. And you excel at closing big deals. You are really best at the high-level stuff: big ideas and solving big problems. The smaller and more detailed things become, the less they interest you. Sound familiar?

Seeing the Future. As a Visionary, you are great with Research and Development (more "R" than "D") for new products and services. You always have a pulse on the market/industry—and even the future needs of clients. You think strategically, always seeing the whole picture and connecting the dots. You see things that others can't. This positions you perfectly to create and champion the company vision. You help the rest of the team understand what's going to be necessary to stay ahead. You are great at turning your best ideas about the future into a vision—as long as you don't have to implement any of those plans. Your vision is so strong, you are convinced the company can get there. Although you don't yet know exactly how, that does not lessen your conviction.

Todd Sachse, the Visionary of Sachse Construction, a $120 million general contractor, made a bold move in 2009 as the great recession descended. He decided to buck the trend of the industry and not downsize in the shrinking market. He believed that the recession would not last forever, so he viewed this as an opportunity to achieve two objectives. He wanted to hire new talent that wouldn't otherwise be available. Plus, he wanted to maintain the vast majority of his staff for when the recession ended. This positioned the company to capitalize on opportunities that other companies couldn't pursue because of their extreme downsizing. As a result, Sachse Construction grew 200% during and coming out of the great recession. During that same time, many other general contractors went out of business or shrank to less than half their previous size.

Because of all these amazing gifts, Visionaries are the creators of almost everything. Very little exists on our planet without the Visionaries of the world. As mentioned at the beginning of this chapter, you are the 3% of the population that creates two-thirds of the new jobs.

A Hunter Mentality. In John F. Dini's book, he calls you "Hunters," meaning that you are wired differently than most. You are always in "hunting" mode. Your type of hunting is for ideas, deals, opportunities, and solutions to big problems. Dini describes you as having "the ability to navigate in the fog," explaining you know "how to keep moving in the right direction when you don't have a compass and there aren't any signposts." He says, "Entrepreneurs [Visionaries] hunt. They don't manage. They explore rather than analyze. They build companies with vision, creativity, and tenacity; not with policies and procedures."

If most or all of what you just read describes you, you are a Visionary. Know thyself and be free!

THE VISIONARY ROLE: HERE'S WHAT YOU DO

The role of the Visionary in an organization is ultimately tailored to their specific Unique Ability®. The most common roles we see the Visionary playing are as follows:

- Entrepreneurial "spark plug"
- Inspirer
- Passion provider
- Developer of new/big ideas/breakthroughs
- Big problem solver

- Engager and maintainer of big external relationships
- Closer of big deals
- Learner, researcher, and discoverer
- Company vision creator and champion

THE VISIONARY DNA: HERE'S WHAT YOU ARE

Our experience also shows a very consistent pattern of traits that are common to a true Visionary. They typically:

- Are the founding entrepreneur.
- Have lots of ideas/idea creation/growth ideas.
- Are strategic thinkers.
- Always see the big picture.
- Have a pulse on the industry and target market.
- Research and develop new products and services.
- Manage big external relationships (e.g., customer, vendor, industry).
- Get involved with customers and employees when vision is needed.
- Inspire people.
- Are creative problem solvers (big problems).
- Create the company vision and protect it.
- Sell and close big deals.
- Connect the dots.
- On occasion do the work, provide the service, make the product.

THE VISIONARY CHALLENGES: HERE'S WHAT YOU AREN'T

Assuming that you now understand these wonderful traits, you might be thinking that Visionaries (perhaps you) are practically superhuman. Right?

Well, like most things in nature—with special gifts come special challenges. So, let's see what special challenges a uniquely gifted Visionary faces. Once again, a good rule of thumb is that if you possess 80% or more of the characteristics discussed in this chapter, you are a Visionary. Actually, you may be quite capable of doing many of the things that follow—you just don't enjoy them enough to keep up with them over time.

Staying Focused. For one, you get bored easily. As a result, you start creating a little chaos, just to spice things up a bit. That pattern shows up even more whenever you step into the Integrator role. Everybody gets excited about your new idea or direction. The organization has this wonderful 90-day spike in performance. Then, unfortunately, everything tends to come crashing down in a heap. And that's because the Visionary in you got bored with the day-to-day redundancy of running the business, literally self-sabotaging your own vision.

One Visionary confessed, "I get bored pretty easily, and my work energy ebbs at times." Another said, "My biggest challenge is boredom. When I find extra capacity and time I tend to meddle, filling this time by getting involved in other people's accountabilities." Yet another said, "I struggle with maintaining focus and following through." You start many different projects at once, while only a few get completed.

Too Many Ideas. Your people love your Visionary learning capability. As a lifetime learner you always need to be figuring stuff out—which you do by doing, in a very hands-on interactive way. This practice, however, can be rather disruptive. You love "breaking the mold" and pursuing the shiny stuff that really doesn't fit with the company's Core Focus. You have little empathy for the negative impact this has on capacity, resources, people, and profitability. As a result, your new idea can actually sabotage your best idea. This may be your Achilles' heel as a Visionary.

Marc Schechter, Visionary and co-owner of Schechter Wealth, a premier investment advisory and advanced life insurance design firm with 40 teammates, stated, "My ever-growing wish list is always bigger than our resources are capable of tackling; it is a challenge for me to conclude with my team which ideas not to act on. I'm also challenged with my new ideas because without proper resources, they will take me away from responsibilities I have in executing the existing plan." Another Visionary, when asked what their biggest challenges are, simply said: "Too many ideas." And another said, "I'm always trying to get 100 pounds of sh*t into a 50-pound bag."

In his book *The Hypomanic Edge: The Link Between (a Little) Craziness and (a Lot of) Success in America*, John D. Gartner imparts an interesting theory about Visionaries: part of their M.O. could be considered a form of mania. Gartner practices psychotherapy and is an associate professor of psychiatry at Johns Hopkins University School of Medicine. His powerful and enlightening book shows that many of the great Visionaries in the past may have been hypomanic. Gartner describes hypomania as a mild form of mania that endows a person with unusual energy, creativity, enthusiasm, and a propensity for taking risks. One notable hypomanic case referenced by Gartner is Andrew Carnegie, who built the American steel industry.

Gartner explains that the reason there are so many entrepreneurs (Visionaries) in America is that most of us are immigrants. It lies in our genes because of our forebears who had the will, optimism, and daring to leave their countries for the "promised land."

Dan Sullivan, the creator of The Strategic Coach program, which has coached over 15,000 entrepreneurs, describes the phenomenon this way: "Entrepreneurs have an unrealistic optimism. It's chemical in the brain. They see things others can't." Along the same lines, Steve Jobs of Apple was once described as having a "reality distortion field."

Whiplash. Another trait we see often is what we refer to as "organizational whiplash." In this case, the organization is so tuned in to the Visionary and your ideas that whenever you turn your head to the right to pursue a new idea, it forces the whole organization to the right. Then, following your natural Visionary instincts, you turn your head in the other direction, toward another idea—and WHIP! The organization tries to snap to the new direction, but it can't keep up with the pace of the head turns. Eventually, they lose all sense of where they are headed. We can't really hold the Visionary at fault for this one. You likely aren't even aware that it's happening—until the damage has been done. This leads to another dynamic that ails many organizations—a lack of consistency.

Along these same lines, we commonly see a sort of binary behavior where you are either all in on something, or out entirely . . . and it changes back and forth—a lot. This effect is similar to someone playing with a light switch: ON-OFF-ON-OFF-ON . . . All of this can create chaos for an organization. Surprised? Or does this sound familiar?

In many cases this indicates some level of ADD. This is actually a gift because it provokes so many ideas. However, on the negative side, you are unable to pay attention to someone speaking to you unless they make their point in under 30 seconds. They don't feel like you care enough to listen. And they may even experience *more* difficulty speaking with you once they anticipate you shutting them down when they can't get their point across quickly enough. You jump from topic to topic, without a segue, making it hard for people to follow you. You think they surely have caught your point, while they may not feel comfortable stopping you to clarify—which they may well need to do a lot. Miscommunication runs rampant. You are frustrated—and so are they.

Sweating the Details. You aren't good at managing and holding people accountable, typically don't like details, don't like running the day-to-day of the business on a long-term basis, and aren't good at following through.

Clearly articulating the details of your vision to others can be quite a challenge. And having to repeat it often wears you out. A great example of how this communication problem is created appears in the book *Made to Stick*, by Chip and Dan Heath. The brothers describe a study that was done at Stanford University. Two students would sit face-to-face. One would be given a list of 25 well-known songs and instructed to pick one and tap out the rhythm on the table for the other, who was supposed to guess the tune. Out of 120 tapped songs, the listeners guessed only three right. This illustrates an amazing point. The person tapping out "Twinkle, Twinkle, Little Star" hears every note perfectly in his head. He is surprised to find out that it's only guessed right 2.5% of the time. He does not realize the listener is only hearing monotonous thumps on the table.

As a Visionary, you have a crystal-clear picture in your mind of what you want. It's in vivid color. When you explain it, you hear the sweet sound of music. Unfortunately, much of the time it comes across to others listening as simply "thump, thump, thump." This comes from *under*-communicating your vision. The same ability that allows you to create a vision is inextricably attached to your lack of ability to communicate it well.

Developing Talent. In *Good to Great*, Jim Collins describes one common leadership behavior pattern as "a genius with a thousand helpers." Many Visionaries suffer from this problem. You are very bright, and likely made it this far largely on your own capabilities—expanding the company from startup to where you are today on your own brute strength. However, what got you here won't get you to the next level. You haven't really needed to leverage the capabilities of others, so it isn't surprising that you've spent little time thinking about how to develop such resources. It is exceedingly difficult for you to attract the type of leadership that could eventually run the day-to-day without you. As an entrepreneur you don't like being told what to do. Your gift is actually telling other people what to do. So, you naturally order your young, high-potential, talented leaders around—and end up running them off instead of developing them.

You may even see your company as a platform from which you can display your brilliance to the world. You are a rock star, and this is your stage. Your company is your identity. This view leaves little space for talent to develop around you.

You are a competitor. While you see this trait positively, being driven to succeed in whatever you undertake, others see a very different side of you. That side makes it very difficult to build a healthy team. When you are aggressive in meetings, it makes you difficult to challenge. When frustrated, you may take a tone of condescension and appear dismissive of those who fall short of your expectations. This behavior can easily discourage healthy debate. It may even encourage the type of sycophants that blind your organization to facing the true issues your team must address in order to grow. Open and honest? Not so much. The team will progressively make fewer and fewer decisions. Why should they risk the chance of being wrong and incurring your wrath? Plus, they know their "genius" is going to make the call anyway.

In an extreme case, one unnamed client complained that her people all knew her "look." Each one had felt the daggers that shot from their leader's eyes whenever they had voiced an opinion that did not closely match her own. A telltale pursing of her lips was immediately followed by an explosion of heated words outlining the stupidity of their comments. The team learned fast, and didn't fall into that trap more than once. They watched new employees naively walk into their own bloody ambush—it was like some cruel form of initiation. Eventually, each member of the team learned to be a good parrot—following the rules and sitting alertly at the table. Meanwhile, she could never understand why she felt so alone on this ship of hers. She lamented that she had no one else on her team as capable as she was. All the time, of course, they simply bit their tongues because they were too afraid to speak up.

Also in *Good to Great*, Jim Collins describes a clear example of a "Rugged Individualist." In the 1960s and 1970s, a classic genius named Henry Singleton built Teledyne from an obscure little company to reach #293 on the Fortune 500 list—in just six years. Growing through aggressive acquisitions, his empire expanded to include 130 different profit centers—ranging from insurance to exotic metals. Henry was the octopus in the middle of it all—holding it together. Incredibly, he was able to do it. When he was 72, he stepped away from day-to-day management duties. He had never given much thought to succession. In less than ten years following his departure, Teledyne's cumulative stock returns unwound—trailing the general stock market by 66%. Was he a success for achieving such heights? Or a failure for not building a great company to last after his departure?

THE VISIONARY DNA: COMMON CHALLENGES

Our experience shows us there is an obvious pattern in the aforementioned Visionary traits that tends to contribute to some of their biggest challenges. Those challenges are as follows:

- Inconsistency
- Organizational "whiplash," the head turn
- Dysfunctional team, a lack of openness and honesty
- Lack of clear direction/under-communication
- Reluctance to let go
- Underdeveloped leaders and managers
- "Genius with a thousand helpers"
- Ego and feelings of value dependent on being needed by others
- Eyes (appetite) bigger than stomach; 100 pounds forced into a 50-pound bag
- Resistance to following standardized processes
- Quickly and easily bored
- No patience for the details
- Amplification of complexity and chaos
- ADD (typical, not always)
- All foot on gas pedal—with no brake
- Drive is too hard for most people

WHAT'S GETTING IN THE WAY?

If you think that you have these unique Visionary talents and aren't sure how to fully maximize them, welcome to the crowd. A lack of Visionary self-awareness is a common pattern. We often see this in working with hundreds of real-life Visionaries. Why didn't they initially see themselves as a true Visionary, or maximize this potential? Three reasons most frequently appear:

1. Role Awareness. You aren't aware that a stand-alone Visionary role exists in an organization. This problem is common in companies that have started from scratch. You have just done everything that was needed—until everything became too much.

Brandon Stallard, for instance, always followed his instincts in business. He built his business, TPS Logistics, from startup to 85 people by following his gut. About 12 years after startup, he learned about the Visionary role. He realized that he was the textbook definition of one, and he was overjoyed that he could spend all of his working time in the role. He clarified the role in his organization and hasn't looked back. Fitting into the role was bumpy at first, and letting go of the day-to-day reins to his Integrator took some practice. Yet his assuming the Visionary role has taken the company to a new level.

2. Ability Awareness. You aren't fully aware of your own natural gifts as a Visionary. Building a company is hard work. You put your nose to the grindstone to make sure the business kept growing. Unfortunately, always just rolling up your sleeves never clarified or helped you see your true genetic encoding.

Matt Rossetti of ROSSETTI, a world-class architectural firm with over 70 employees, always did what came naturally to him. He knew his tendencies were unusual compared to most. He always had the ability to see the big picture, come up with great creative solutions to big problems, and inspire his team.

Says Matt, "I never realized I was a Visionary. It came slowly and gradually to me, almost as a result of finding out what I don't do well. Once I realized I was a Visionary (others saw it long before I did), I was enormously motivated and freed to really grow and be courageous in the role . . . which it requires! I began to turn everything that wasn't for a Visionary over to our Integrator. We have taken the company to another level!"

Still, Matt was reluctant "about being anointed as Visionary." As he said, "It is such a sacred role. While some jump right into it, others might be more reluctant and need to be pushed in that direction. I'll bet many good potential Visionaries miss out on the value of the role because of that."

3. Letting Go. Your need for control, or a lack of trust, is keeping you from letting go enough to embrace the Visionary role. Like many entrepreneurs, you may be good at multiple roles. You know how to run the company—because you've always had to. What happens, though, when your hands aren't big enough to hang on to it all? Of course letting go requires trust. The tools and rules we will teach you in this book will enable you to develop that trust with your Integrator. In turn, you'll be confident that things won't come crashing down when you finally do let go.

One Visionary (who will remain unnamed) runs a very successful company. On the outside he seems to be fine. He has won all sorts of awards and accolades. Inside the company, however, things are chaotic. The organization is marked by a lack of accountability and consistency. His people are tired from all the fits and starts, and he is burning out. He knows something has to give, but he fears relinquishing the day-to-day control to someone else. As a result he's carrying the entire load. This state of affairs can't last forever, but as long as it does, the company is going to be filled with internal chaos.

Regardless of which of the abovementioned reasons you might be facing for not fully embracing your role as Visionary, you will find solutions in this book.

YOU ARE HERE

So, there you are, our hero the Visionary—all alone at the helm of your business. You are frustrated, you are doing everything, and you're burning out. You're suffering from what we call the Five Frustrations:

1. **Lack of Control.** You started this business so you could have more control over your time, money, and freedom—your future. Once you reach a certain point of growth, however, you realize that somehow you actually have *less* control over these things than you've ever had before. The business is now controlling you!

2. **Lack of Profit.** Quite simply, you don't have enough. It's a frustrating feeling to look at the monthly P&L (or daily cash flow) and realize that no matter how hard you work, the numbers just don't add up.

3. **People.** Nobody (employees, partners, vendors) seems to understand you or do things your way. You're just not on the same page.

4. **Hitting the Ceiling.** Growth has stopped. The business is more complex, and you can't figure out exactly why it isn't working.

5. **Nothing Is Working.** You've tried several remedies, consulted books, and instituted quick fixes. None of these have worked for long. Your employees have become numb to new initiatives. Your wheels are spinning—and you have no traction.

To compound the difficulties, you are now bored with the repetition of day-to-day execution. Your company has outgrown the stage where force of will could solve almost any challenge. You feel like you're coaxing a cat to swim across a pond—it's just not a natural thing for a Visionary. It's time to seriously address the company's structure, people, and process. So now what?

THE SOLUTION: EMBRACE YOUR VISIONARY NATURE

Not all Visionary entrepreneurs are frustrated. Many have engineered significant growth, feel in control, have enviable profits, and employ people who work together as a team. Instead of the endless issues that cause the minor distractions so common to many companies, these Visionaries run businesses that are focused, consistent, and healthy. You can get everything you want from your business. If you are willing to do what it takes to be your best, there is hope.

If you are a Visionary, you must delegate the role of implementing your ideas in order to elevate yourself to your true talents. This will free up your energy and creativity to grow your company, protect your vision, wow your customers, protect your culture, and stay three steps ahead of everyone—including the competition.

At Uckele Health and Nutrition (UHN), Visionary Mike Uckele decided to hire an Integrator. This was six years after taking over ownership of the family business from his father and uncle. He had doubled the size of the company over that period, playing both roles. He knew he was not good at executing the details, but wanted to wait until he could afford to hire an executive. Four years ago he named Del Collins as Integrator, and UHN has grown 20% per year to $23 million and 108 people. Del was promoted from within after two years of working for the company. Mike describes the results of the decision as "Very rewarding. It allows me to no longer burn the candle at both ends and worry about everything getting completed. I spend more time with family and friends, and focus solely on growing the business." He describes his role as "the facilitator of creative ideas and relationship builder."

As the old proverb so accurately notes, "Vision without execution is just hallucination." In other words, you need someone to help you execute your vision. The idea isn't enough: it must be implemented to have value. It's your choice. For those of you who are searching for answers, let's get to work.

Tens of thousands of Visionaries have been where you are now. Some have failed, but many have gone to the next level. They just didn't do it alone. You will now have to decide. Are you willing to delegate and elevate?

After all, Ray Kroc couldn't have done it without Fred Turner at McDonald's. Henry Ford couldn't have done it without James Couzens at Ford. Joel Pearlman couldn't have done it without Rob Dube at imageOne. John Pollock couldn't have done it without Paul Boyd at Financial Gravity.

Now you see the landscape for the Visionary. The powers and the pitfalls. All of these Visionaries stood where you are standing right now, and they made a choice. In the words of Randy Pruitt, Visionary of Randall Industries, one of the largest radiator manufacturing and distribution companies in North America, "If you are looking to grow your company, you can't do it without an Integrator. At some point you will have to relieve the weight carried on your shoulders and find someone to carry it with you."

The Visionary DNA

Common Roles	Common Traits	Common Challenges
• Entrepreneurial "spark plug" • Inspirer • Passion provider • Developer of new/big ideas/ breakthroughs	• Are the founding entrepreneur • Have lots of ideas/ idea creation/idea growth • Are strategic thinkers	• Inconsistency • Organizational "whiplash," the head turn • Dysfunctional team, a lack of openness and honesty

	The Visionary DNA *(continued)*	
Common Roles	**Common Traits**	**Common Challenges**
• Big problem solver • Engager and maintainer of big external relationships • Closer of big deals • Learner, researcher, and discoverer • Company vision creator and champion	• Always see the big picture • Have a pulse on the industry and target market • Research and develop new products and services • Manage big external relationships (e.g., customer, vendor, industry) • Get involved with customers and employees when Visionary is needed • Inspire people • Are creative problem solvers (big problems) • Create the company vision and protect it • Sell and close big deals • Connect the dots • On occasion do the work, provide the service, make the product	• Lack of clear direction/under-communication • Reluctance to let go • Underdeveloped leaders and managers • "Genius with a thousand helpers" • Ego and feelings of value dependent on being needed by others • Eyes (appetite) bigger than stomach; 100 pounds in a 50-pound bag • Resistance to following standardized processes • Quickly and easily bored • No patience for the details • Amplification of complexity and chaos • ADD (typical; not always) • All foot on gas pedal—with no brake • Drive is too hard for most people

Before we discuss the Integrator role, please take the assessment below to see if you are truly a Visionary. Also consider having your Leadership Team complete it on your behalf. The Visionary Indicator Assessment is also available online at www.rocketfuelnow.com.

VISIONARY INDICATOR ASSESSMENT

For each statement below, rank yourself on a scale of 1 to 5, where 1 rarely describes you and 5 almost always describes you:

#	Statement	1	2	3	4	5
1	I have an affinity for tackling and creatively solving the biggest, most complex problems.	1	2	3	4	5
2	I am constantly generating new ideas. I never run out.	1	2	3	4	5
3	I am a great leader. People tend to follow me.	1	2	3	4	5
4	I am highly optimistic in my outlook.	1	2	3	4	5
5	My natural perspective is oriented toward things that are external to the company, big-picture or futuristic thinking.	1	2	3	4	5
6	I am the creator of, and champion for, the company Vision.	1	2	3	4	5
7	I sometimes find it difficult to translate my Vision into something that others understand. They don't seem to get it.	1	2	3	4	5

8	I eventually have the "right" idea, and know it. It may come from having a large volume of different ideas or a small number that I feel strongly about.	1	2	3	4	5
9	I have zero patience for putting operational policy, structure, and repeatability systems in place.	1	2	3	4	5
10	I naturally think about the future of the industry, our product or our service, what's coming, and how we can best position the company to take advantage of it.	1	2	3	4	5
11	I am naturally insightful, skilled at deductive reasoning, and highly innovative in thinking of ways to make ideas bigger and better.	1	2	3	4	5
12	I don't like being held accountable or being told what to do. I find it challenging to establish genuine accountability in my company.	1	2	3	4	5
13	I embrace and enjoy the role of being the engine for big, new, breakthrough ideas, the spark, getting them started.	1	2	3	4	5
14	I embrace and enjoy the role of solving the biggest problems faced by the company.	1	2	3	4	5
15	I embrace and enjoy the role of being responsible for a few large, key, strategic relationships (vendor, client, banking, industry).	1	2	3	4	5

(Continued on next page)

16	I embrace and enjoy the role of selling and closing big deals.	1	2	3	4	5	
17	I struggle with follow-through. I lose interest in finishing new ideas. I don't have patience or interest for a lot of detail. I wish people would get to the point. I get bored and distracted very easily.	1	2	3	4	5	
18	I embrace and enjoy the role of being the "entrepreneurial spark plug," providing passion and inspiration.	1	2	3	4	5	
19	I embrace and enjoy the role of researching and developing new products and services.	1	2	3	4	5	
20	I embrace and enjoy the role of leading the way on learning and discovery that advances the organization.	1	2	3	4	5	
	COUNT: Total number of each ranking						
		x1	x2	x3	x4	x5	
	TOTAL: Multiply by number above						

Add all five numbers from the TOTAL line above to determine your **Visionary Indicator Score:** _____ (A VIS of 80 or more is considered strong.)

CHAPTER 2

THE INTEGRATOR

Where your talents and the needs of the world cross, there lies your calling, vocation, or purpose—paraphrasing the ideas of Aristotle in *Politics*. It is important to believe that Integrators truly do walk the earth. Making someone else's vision happen is a very noble calling, vocation, or purpose.

An Integrator's role and skills are quite unique. For an organization, they are the glue, the Visionary's right hand; they beat the drum and make sure the trains run on time. You may hear them referred to as #2, inside man, president, COO, general manager, or chief of staff. Who is the Integrator in your organization? Are you an Integrator?

Let's clarify the Integrator function and the value it will provide your organization. Every organization must have someone playing the Integrator role to truly build a company to the next level. Let's explore what life looks like for an Integrator.

HERE'S WHAT INTEGRATORS BRING TO AN ORGANIZATION

An Integrator is a person who has the Unique Ability® to harmoniously integrate the major functions of the business, run the organization, and manage the day-to-day issues that arise. The Integrator is the glue that holds the people, processes, systems, priorities, and strategy of the company together. We use the term "Integrator" to describe the role more accurately than other common external titles such as president, COO, general manager, or chief of staff. Integrator is simply the best word to describe this position.

The following characteristics are typical Integrator representations. No Integrator has 100% of them. A person that has 80% or more of these qualities is very likely an Integrator.

Running the Day-to-Day. In contrast to Visionaries, Integrators are typically very good at leading, managing, and holding people accountable. They love running the day-to-day aspects of the business. They enjoy being accountable for profit and loss, and for the execution of the business plan. They remove obstacles so that people can execute. Typically, they operate at a more detailed level than their Visionary counterparts. When a major initiative is undertaken, the Integrator will foresee the ripple of implications that will move across the organization as a result. Visionaries typically don't even see, or will substantially underestimate, these ripple effects.

Larry G. Linne, along with co-author Ken Koller, describes the value of an Integrator in their book *Make the Noise Go Away: The Power of an Effective Second in*

Command. The business fable describes an owner (Visionary) who started his business because he wanted the freedom that comes with owning your own company, only to find out that the business can end up owning you. Hiring a second-in-command (Integrator) finally freed up the owner (Visionary) to truly achieve the freedom he sought. The book describes all of the routine details that a Visionary can get stuck with as "noise." A great second-in-command (Integrator) can make all of that noise go away.

When Keith Walters joined Ron Johnsey at Axiometrics, a 28-person analytics firm, the combination literally changed their world. A longtime veteran of his industry, Ron could see the future like few others. This ability had enabled Axiometrics to develop market-leading solutions to support a variety of decisions concerning multi-family commercial real estate. Yet as the firm grew, Ron had less and less time to spend looking down the road. He found himself in "head down" mode most of the time. He had to react to various developments far more often than he was able to make proactive moves to anticipate what he saw coming down the pike.

Once Keith became his Integrator, a huge burden was lifted from Ron's shoulders. Operational matters that would take Ron hours to resolve took Keith a fraction of that time. Keith was much better suited to handling those matters than Ron. Keith even seemed to enjoy them! Ron was thrilled to let them go—along with all their related noise.

In this newfound quiet, Ron rekindled his flame for seeking the future in their market. His fountain of ideas sprang anew, and before long a few of those moonshot-level ideas were transformed into practical initiatives. With Keith's added discipline, Ron's creative energy was harnessed into a powerful strategic plan—with deliberate actions and accountabilities to keep the plan consistently moving forward. Ron and Keith are playing squarely in their respective sweet spots. As a result, the company is performing at record-breaking levels of achievement. The organization is ablaze with all this newfound energy.

The Steady Force. An Integrator is the type of person who is obsessed about organizational clarity. They are great at making sure people are communicating within the organization.

Integrators are fanatical about resolution and forcing conclusions. When the team is at odds, they are a masterful tiebreaker. They drive everyone to execute the business plan. They are great at managing big organizational projects. They are masters of follow-through. When priorities need to be set for the organization and everyone must be aligned with those priorities, they are right at home keeping everyone laser focused and driving results. They create organizational focus and accountability.

Integrators have a unique skill to execute a vision. They provide a cadence and a consistency for the team, and help them stick with it. Think of the consistent drumbeat on an ancient ship, or the coxswain in a crew shouting "row . . . row . . . row . . ." These verbal cues influence speed, timing, and coordination. They enable everyone to pull together in the same direction. An Integrator is that steady force for the organization.

An Integrator harmoniously integrates the major functions of the business (e.g., sales, marketing, operations, and finance). When those major functions are strong, and you have strong people accountable for each function, healthy tension is created. The Integrator blends that friction into greater energy for the company as a whole. At the same time, that creates unity that leads to a healthy, functional leadership team.

Integrators create organizational lucidity, enabling the right hand to know what the left hand is doing—keeping everyone in sync. They have a gift for doing what we call "getting all of the arrows pointing in the same direction." The best way to describe what that means is to imagine all of the people in your organization as arrows. Think about the direction they are pointing based on their interpretation of the values, priorities, key issues—basically what is most important to the company. If your people are not all on the same page with these items, the arrows will be pointing in many different directions. Some of your arrows are pointing up, some down, right, left, or diagonally. As a result, your organization is literally stuck or moving so slowly that brute force is required to achieve your goals.

Now imagine all of those arrows pointing in one single direction. Everyone's goals, values, and priorities aligned. The result will be your organization moving forward freely and effortlessly. The Integrator has the powerful ability to point a group of people all in the same direction.

Ellyn Davidson, Integrator and managing partner at Brogan & Partners, a 40-person marketing communications firm, describes this incredible ability in an all-encompassing quote. "As an Integrator, I lead the agency management team. My primary job is to keep the team focused on reaching our goals, delivering a quality product, keeping our clients happy, and growing our knowledgebase. Our product is only as strong as the collaborative talent, drive, and motivation within Brogan & Partners, so I focus on making sure we all live and breathe our Core Values. I work hard to make sure that we have a dedicated staff that feels appreciated and takes great pride in our work. It's about continuously developing new ways of solving problems and making sure those new solutions are executed and communicated throughout the organization."

The Voice of Reason. The Integrator also filters all of the Visionary's ideas, which helps to eliminate hurdles, stumbling blocks, and barriers for the leadership team.

We found a great father/daughter founding V/I combination at Complete Pharmacy Care, where Leonard Lynskey is the Visionary and Amy Guinan is the Integrator. Leonard's never-ending stream of new ideas was beginning to really challenge the organization until Amy was able to step into the Integrator role. As the Integrator, she filters Leonard's creative genius to help focus him on his best ideas. Leonard feels free. Amy enjoys driving the bus. Together they are creating unprecedented growth for the firm.

A more famous family V/I combo, in this case brothers, is Walt and Roy Disney of the Disney empire. Millions of people are familiar with the incredible Visionary Walt Disney, but few have heard of Roy, and he liked it that way. In fact, he was a partner and co-founder of Disney. Walt was described as the creative man, and Roy was the guy who kept the business stable. In Bob Thomas' *Building a*

Company: Roy O. Disney and the Creation of an Entertainment Empire, Walt is quoted saying, "If it hadn't been for my big brother, I swear I'd've been in jail several times for checks bouncing. I never knew what was in the bank. He kept me on the straight and narrow."

Thomas explains, "Long before Walt produced his first movie cartoon, he looked to Roy for counsel and sympathy. As business partners, Walt was the inventive dreamer, Roy the financial wizard." Roy was described as rejecting the publicity and fame that came with being Walt's brother. He was also camera shy. Yet if not for Roy, would Disney, only one of many animation outfits at the time, have become an empire?

If what you just read describes someone you know, he is an Integrator. If what you just read describes *you*, you are an Integrator—and it's important to know that you have a unique and very valuable place in the world.

THE INTEGRATOR ROLE: HERE'S WHAT YOU DO

Said in a more simplified manner, a great Integrator creates the following results in an organization. Where you see these results showing up, you'll find an Integrator:

- Clarity
- Communication
- Resolution
- Focus
- Accountability

- Team unity
- Well-managed projects
- Follow-through
- Tiebreakers that keep things moving
- No obstacles or barriers
- Prioritization
- Execution
- Steady force/cadence/consistency
- "Glue" holding everything together
- Consistent beating of the drum ("row, row")
- P&L results achieved
- The business plan executed
- The leadership team harmoniously integrated
- Leadership, management, and accountability for the leadership team
- The company operating system being followed by all
- All the arrows pointed in the same direction
- Visionary ideas being harnessed: "Visionary Prozac"
- Day-to-day tasks run smoothly

THE INTEGRATOR DNA: HERE'S WHAT YOU ARE

Our experience also shows a very consistent pattern of positive traits and competencies that are common to Integrators. They are as follows:

- Personally accountable
- Adept at self-management
- Decisive
- Good at planning and organizing
- Strong leader and manager
- Effective conflict manager
- Catalyst for team cohesion
- Goal achiever
- Conceptual thinker
- Employee developer/coach
- Resilient
- Adaptable
- Able to understand and evaluate others
- Forward thinking
- Problem-solver
- Persuasive
- Continuous learner

THE INTEGRATOR CHALLENGES: HERE'S WHAT YOU AREN'T

As an Integrator you might be thumping your chest by this time, but you should be aware that with special gifts come special challenges. Here are the challenges an Integrator faces, along with the downsides of being one.

No Glory. For one, Integrators are the unsung heroes. Not much is written about them, and they have to be okay with that. Many books and articles have been written on Visionaries, but very few on Integrators.

One great example of such an unsung hero is Fred Turner of McDonald's. Most have heard of Ray Kroc, the Visionary who put the hamburger chain on the map, and much has been written about him. Conversely, you can find very little written on Fred Turner. He was hired as a grill man for Kroc's very first franchise. Within three years he was Ray's right-hand man. Fred is credited with the fanatical consistency in executing the franchise plan. He wrote the "bible," as the franchise-training manual was called. He is the creator of "Hamburger U," the franchise-training program that is now appropriately called the Fred L. Turner Training Center. Fred became Operations Manager in 1958 with 34 restaurants. By the time he retired in 2004, the company had expanded to 31,500 restaurants—and billions served, yet very few people knew him for all he did.

Being the Pessimist. Integrators are often deemed as "glass is half empty" kind of people. This accusation most often comes from your Visionary, by the way. A good Integrator is able to poke holes in ideas, opportunities, and potential solutions. As a result, you can come off as being a pessimist or negative.

A lot of times you have to be the bad guy. You have to say "no" often. You must make the tough calls when the team is divided on an important issue. You are the one who has to filter the Visionary's many ideas. You must convince him when the idea doesn't fit with the company's Core Focus or the timing isn't right.

Discipline and Accountability. You are the one who delivers the bad news to employees. You're in charge of the dirty work that needs to be done. Many times you are the one making the tough personnel decisions and delivering the news, whether that's firing a long-term employee, demoting someone who can't keep up, or having a last-straw conversation with a problematic team member. All of these duties put you in a position where you are frequently disliked by someone for something.

As Curtis Burstein, Integrator at Etkin Equities, describes this not-so-pleasant part of his job, "When there is a breakdown and someone doesn't belong on the bus, I have to make the tough decision and let them go."

The bad-guy role can wear on you and cause you to be short, callous, or downright mean. Sometimes, being so far down into the weeds, you start to lose sight of the big picture and the "people/human" side of the operation. You can feel unappreciated at times and become unappreciative of your people. You aren't getting thank-yous, so you stop giving them to others.

As the person who harmoniously integrates the leadership team, you are constantly dealing with friction. This affects your energy and you can become frustrated and tense. In this frame of mind you don't make decisions with the same effectiveness. People see that you are frustrated, and it affects the culture.

Going Slow to Go Fast. You are often accused of moving too slowly by your Visionary. Therefore, you are constantly wrestling with balancing the speed at which the Visionary wants to move new initiatives through the organization against the limited resources available to execute them. As Del Collins at Uckele Health and Nutrition puts it, "One of my biggest challenges is moving at the speed of vision. Typically a vision can be seen long before you get there. I am challenged to balance the idea-to-reality timing so that both are satisfied."

Lack of Appreciation. The toughest one of all is that your job can be downright lonely. As an Integrator you are in a position that doesn't allow for a lot of pats on the back, small talk, and friendships. Oftentimes, the better you are at doing your job, the less you are noticed. In the words of one Integrator, "It's a relatively thankless job. Don't get me wrong; I know I'm appreciated. But there are a lot of things that get done behind the scenes that no one would notice. Sometimes I feel like I'm the only one who knows I'm holding things together, because it's done behind the scenes. That can be lonely at times."

Not Superman. You see what needs to get done, and you wish it could all be done right now. You really want to bring order to the chaos. Lots of others are counting on you, and it hurts to think about letting them down. At times, these thoughts will blend together and convince you to rationalize some unreasonable expectations of yourself. Too much. Too soon. Too fast. You expect a lot from yourself—sometimes too much. And when you can't deliver on it all, you beat yourself up.

THE INTEGRATOR DNA: COMMON CHALLENGES

The Integrator traits from our experience that can be construed as negative and pessimistic include a selection that speaks to the downsides of their role and their need for a Visionary complement. A summary of those challenges is as follows:

- The job can be thankless
- Accusations of pessimism
- Being considered negative by others, as the "hole poker"
- Loneliness
- Constant friction and tension
- Frustration balancing so many resources
- Being the bearer of bad news, as the "bad guy"
- Having to do the dirty work (firing people)
- Lack of recognition
- Having to say "no" a lot
- Being accused of moving too slowly
- Setting the bar too high on self/unrealistic expectations of self

WHAT'S GETTING IN THE WAY?

At this point we hope to have made the Integrator role very clear, as well as its value. Assuming we have, then what's the gap between where you are and where you could be? We most commonly see three scenarios when an Integrator role is not fully functioning:

1. Ineffectiveness. You currently have an Integrator, but it isn't working. The lines of responsibility are crossed, and the relationship is not as productive as it should be.

The three founding partners of a health services company with 45 employees and $8 million in revenue eventually agreed on which one of them had the Unique Ability® to fill the role of Integrator. This represented a big departure from the tribunal decision-making process they'd always used.

As owners, each of them felt entitled/obligated to weigh in on pretty much every decision being made in the company. From their perspective, sending out directives worked pretty well. However, the rest of the organization had quite a different view. The employees were confused about the plan, torn between whose approval they should seek, and generally hesitant to raise issues that might be controversial.

An additional point of concern was that the owners found that team members were acting in the same way our children often do. If a team member didn't like the answer she got from one owner, she'd simply go ask another one. That led to lots of false starts and wasted energy, along with a healthy dose of political friction throughout the ranks.

Clarifying the Integrator role was a big step toward streamlining accountability and communication. As a result of making one person accountable, the organization has become much more nimble. Clarity has the troops feeling much better about the direction of the firm. And the founding partners are now getting along better than they ever have. Says one, "We've finally put that three-headed monster behind us!"

2. Lack of Awareness. You may have an Integrator in your organization, but you just don't know it yet. Someone on your team may already have precisely the set of capabilities you need for your Integrator. You've just been so busy making things happen that you simply haven't noticed.

Once Matt Rossetti realized his genetic encoding was to be a Visionary, the next step was finding his perfect Integrator match. Fortunately, he did not have to look far, as that person was right under his nose. Dave Richards, a principal in the company, was a textbook integrator. Dave had been with the organization for over 30 years. Once the role was described to the leadership team, everyone said, "Dave, you should be the Integrator." Matt was a little reluctant to let go and admit he couldn't run the whole show, but after a very short time they realized they were the perfect V/I match.

3. Nonexistence. You don't have one in your organization. Therefore, you will need to go outside to find one.

John Pollock is a classic Visionary, and he quickly grasped the value of having an Integrator. Spurred along by stories from entrepreneur friends who had successfully put an Integrator in place, he was anxious to enjoy the benefits himself. He looked around his organization and realized that he simply did not have one anywhere among his current team. He then reached out to his extensive network of contacts for possibilities. In short order, he reconnected with someone from the earlier days of his career, Paul Boyd—who fit a prototypical Integrator profile. Paul stepped into the role and immediately began the process of restoring order to various areas of the firm.

John gave Paul the space to use his gift. Meanwhile, John, who has a never-ending flow of energy, directed his attention solely to those Visionary activities he loves the most—and that only he could provide for the firm. This resulted in new service offerings and powerful new content for marketing. A series of breakthrough leaps forward soon followed.

THE SOLUTION: V+I. PUTTING THE TWO PIECES TOGETHER

So, there is our Integrator. Capable, yet incomplete without a Visionary complement. Like an Oreo cookie without the cream filling. So what now?

If you are a Visionary forced to play the Integrator role because you're stuck with nobody to free you up, the first step is to search for someone in your organization. If the right person can't be found in your organization, you must look outside. (How to do this is coming up in Chapter 6.) In the meantime, you must play the Integrator role on a temporary basis, to the best of your ability. One Visionary client made a funny comment about temporarily having to fill the Integrator seat. "If I have to do that, I'll feel like more of a *Dis-Integrator*." While the remark was made in humor, that client was in fact calling a spade a spade. At least that Visionary gained better clarity about what the Integrator really could do for his organization.

If you are partners co-running your business, often one of you is an Integrator and the other is a Visionary. If you are both running the business, this usually causes confusion for both you and your people. If you will divide and conquer, you will create clarity, execute better, and reach your goals faster.

In these first two chapters we have painted a vivid picture of how a typical Visionary and Integrator function in an organization. As we move forward to the remaining chapters, we will address the A to Z of how to maximize this powerful relationship.

The Integrator DNA

Common Roles	Common Traits	Common Challenges
• Communication • Resolution • Focus • Accountability • Team unity • Well-managed projects • Follow-through • Tiebreakers that keep things moving • No obstacles or barriers • Prioritization • Execution • Steady force/ cadence/ consistency • "Glue" holding everything together • Consistent beating of the drum ("row, row")	• Personally accountable • Adept at self management • Decisive • Good at planning and organizing • Strong leader and manager • Effective conflict manager • Catalyst for team cohesion • Goal achiever • Conceptual thinker • Employee developer/coach • Resilient • Adaptable • Able to understand and evaluate others • Forward thinking	• The job can be thankless • Accusations of pessimism • Being considered negative by others, as the "hole poker" • Loneliness • Constant friction and tension • Frustration balancing so many resources • Being seen as the "bad guy" . . . bearer of bad news . . . • Having to do the dirty work (firing people) • Lack of recognition

(Continued on next page)

		The Integrator DNA *(continued)*
Common Roles	Common Traits	Common Challenges
• P&L results achieved • The business plan executed • The leadership team harmoniously integrated • Leadership, management, and accountability for the leadership team • The company operating system being followed by all • All the arrows pointed in the same direction • Visionary ideas being harnessed: "Visionary Prozac" • Day-to-day tasks run smoothly	• Problem-solver • Persuasive • Continuous learner	• Having to say "no" a lot • Being accused of moving too slowly • Setting the bar too high on self/unrealistic expectations of self

Please take the Integrator Indicator Assessment on the following page to see if you are truly an Integrator. Have others who know you well take it to see how they view your abilities. If you are a Visionary, use this assessment to score your Integrator candidates. The Integrator Indicator Assessment is also available on our website at www. rocketfuelnow.com.

INTEGRATOR INDICATOR ASSESSMENT

For each statement below, rank yourself on a scale of 1 to 5 where 1 rarely describes you, and 5 almost always describes you:

1	I am adept at quickly identifying and articulating problems, bottlenecks, disconnects, roadblocks, and barriers.	1	2	3	4	5
2	I am great at taking ideas and effectively initializing plans to make them a reality.	1	2	3	4	5
3	I am a great manager of people.	1	2	3	4	5
4	I get accused of being a pessimist and "hole poker."	1	2	3	4	5
5	My natural perspective is oriented toward things that are internal to the company. Getting the house in order/ship-shape.	1	2	3	4	5
6	I am good at (and get a rush out of) being provided with a company Vision, and then turning it into something real.	1	2	3	4	5
7	I am really good at translating someone's Vision into something others can understand and get on board with—laying a solid foundation for execution.	1	2	3	4	5
8	I am great at choosing which options are the best priorities for the organization.	1	2	3	4	5

(Continued on next page)

9	I recognize the need for operational policy, structures, and repeatability to make the Vision a reality. I am able to define meaningful rules and put them in place—without slowing things down and while improving efficiency.	1	2	3	4	5
10	I naturally think about the present, what needs to happen now, and how to keep everything on track for the future vision.	1	2	3	4	5
11	I am naturally analytical, skilled at deductive reasoning, and highly adept at implementing solutions.	1	2	3	4	5
12	I am comfortable being held accountable, and holding others accountable. I see the value in creating the infrastructure for accountability across the organization and am comfortable putting this in place.	1	2	3	4	5
13	I embrace and enjoy the role of executing and delivering P&L results.	1	2	3	4	5
14	I embrace and enjoy the role of providing leadership, management, and accountability for the company's Leadership Team.	1	2	3	4	5
15	I embrace and enjoy the role of effectively integrating all the major functions of the organization.	1	2	3	4	5

16	I embrace and enjoy the role of effectively resolving cross-functional issues, making sure they are harmoniously integrated and orchestrated.	1	2	3	4	5
17	I embrace and enjoy the role of ensuring adherence to the organization's core processes and operating system.	1	2	3	4	5
18	I embrace and enjoy the role of ensuring the organization is aligned with the company's Core Values.	1	2	3	4	5
19	I love running the day-to-day of the business, and take great pride in "making sure the trains run on time."	1	2	3	4	5
20	I embrace and enjoy the role of ensuring the communication is effectively flowing across the organization.	1	2	3	4	5
	COUNT: Total number for each ranking					
		x1	x2	x3	x4	x5
	TOTAL: Multiply by the number above					

Add all five numbers from the TOTAL line above to determine your **Integrator Indicator Score:** _____ (An IIS score of 80 or more is considered strong.)

CHAPTER 3

THE RELATIONSHIP

Yin meet Yang.

The ancient Chinese concept of Yin and Yang describes how two forces that are seemingly contrary to each other—polar opposites—are actually interconnected and interdependent, giving rise to each other as they interact together. They are complementary forces coming together to form a dynamic system wherein the whole is greater than the individual parts. Both are always present, although one may show up more strongly at any given time. They are always opposite and equal.

One without the other is doomed, as humanity with only men or only women could not survive. Together they create—the interaction gives birth. They transform each other via complement. A rope with two twisted strands is much stronger than simply twice the strength of a single strand.

The Visionary and the Integrator go together in the same fashion. It's the perfect combination that spurs companies to greatness.

Ernst & Young conducts an annual Entrepreneur of the Year competition. David Kohl, a principal in the Dallas firm Roach Howard Smith & Barton, is actively involved in the nomination process. In this role he interacts with many entrepreneurial leaders across a broad spectrum of industries. In our discussion, he made a very interesting observation regarding the 65 candidate companies they considered for the award this past year. He noted that all of them had what he called a "pair of leaders" to which he largely attributed their success. Once he learned about the terms Visionary and Integrator, he agreed that this seemed to offer a logical explanation for the superior performance he observed in reviewing these entrepreneurial companies.

HOW V/I RELATIONSHIPS BEGIN

Typically, the Visionary and Integrator relationships emerge along one of four paths:

1. They are co-founders. In this partnership, two people start a company, and most of the time, one partner is naturally the Visionary and the other is the Integrator. Their natural dynamic—along with a lot of hard work, blood, sweat, and tears—elevates the company to greater heights.

One example of two people who co-founded a company and grew it to success is Keith Meadows and John Glover of RepWorx, a successful food and maintenance supplies broker. The two joined forces ten years ago, and the startup has enjoyed rapid growth since day one—capitalizing on the fact that Keith is a textbook Visionary and John a textbook Integrator.

2. They are partners. In situations where a company has more than two partners—either because more than two people founded the company or because additional partners were added later (e.g., mergers, acquisitions, new investors)—it is important to understand that only two of these partners can become the V/I duo. We'll talk more in Chapter 4 about why this is important, and how to make it happen.

In the case of co-founders Scott Bade and James Leneschmidt of ImageSoft, they have a third partner and co-founder who took the entrepreneurial leap together to start ImageSoft—Steve Glisky, who heads up their government practice. Steve is happy to let his two partners assume the Visionary and Integrator roles while he continues operating in his own Unique Ability®. He has the benefit of doing what he loves, letting his partners do what they love, and sharing in the profits the company generates. This also eliminates any organizational confusion created by multiple partners running around shooting orders at people. Everyone in the organization clearly knows each partner's role and responsibility.

3. An existing internal team member becomes the Integrator. ROSSETTI, the architectural firm mentioned before, is a second-generation family business. Ten years after Matt Rossetti took the reins, he realized he had to find an Integrator. Fortunately, his search process was very simple. Dave Richards, a born Integrator, was already a member of Matt's leadership team. Since Dave's promotion to Integrator three years ago, ROSSETTI has enjoyed rapid growth and an incredibly strong culture.

4. The Integrator is hired from the outside. When there is not a natural Integrator among the Founders or Partners, and no candidate exists inside the organization, the Integrator needs to be hired from the outside.

Randy Pruitt of Randall Industries had grown his business from $200K in sales to $8.5 million, standing at the helm the whole way. At a crucial point he anticipated a 40% growth the following year. He knew he would have to grow his team, but didn't know exactly how. Luckily, he met David Bitel through a common associate. David had worked as an Integrator for a prior company, so he explained to Randy what that function does and how that position provides the means for a Visionary like Randy to achieve his growth goals. With David as his Integrator, Randy has doubled the size of the company in five short years.

"HAM AND EGGING IT"

In golf, when two partners are playing well together, it is called "Ham and Egging it." When one partner hits a bad shot, the other hits a great shot—they cover each other. This is what a great V/I team does. They Ham and Egg it!

There's no denying that there is a real chemistry when it's right. Just like Rocket Fuel, there's a chemical mixture that happens—and the result is a powerful expansion of force. When this force is properly focused, it's literally capable of launching you into orbit.

In his book *Start With Why: How Great Leaders Inspire Everyone to Take Action*, Simon Sinek validates this powerful V/I impact on businesses. He describes the two roles as WHY people and HOW people, where the Visionary is the WHY-type and the Integrator is the HOW-type. He explains, "For every great leader, every WHY-type, there is an inspired HOW-type . . . who [can] take the intangible cause and build the infrastructure that can give it life. That infrastructure is what actually makes any measurable change or success possible." He goes on to write, "In every case of a great charismatic leader who ever achieved anything of significance, there was always a person or small group lurking in the shadows that knew HOW to take the vision and make it a reality."

Sinek goes on to share, "WHY-types are the Visionaries, the ones with the overactive imaginations. They tend to be optimists who believe that all the things they imagine can actually be accomplished. HOW-types live more in the here and now. They are the realists and have a clearer sense of all things practical. WHY-types are focused on the things most people can't see, like the future. HOW-types are focused on the things that most people can see, and tend to be better at building structures and processes and getting things done. One is not better than the other, they are just different ways people naturally see and experience the world."

Sinek makes the further point that HOW-types have a strength of ego to admit they are not Visionaries themselves. Rather, they are inspired by the Visionary leader's vision and know how to bring that vision to life. He states, "The best HOW-types generally do not want to be out in front . . . they prefer to work behind the scenes . . . [to] make the vision a reality." He goes on to say that "[i]t takes the combined skill and effort of both for great things to happen." In his book he cites the historical combinations of Bill Gates and Paul Allen at Microsoft, Herb Kelleher and Rollin King at Southwest Airlines, and Steve Jobs and Steve Wozniak at Apple.

"WHY-guys, for all their vision and imagination, often get the short end of the stick. Without someone inspired by their vision and the knowledge to make it a reality, most WHY-types end up as starving visionaries, people with all the answers but never accomplishing much themselves," says Sinek.

One of the most famous businessmen in American history, John D. Rockefeller, knew this truth very well. Although it is almost forgotten in the sands of time, Rockefeller formed a highly successful V/I duo with Henry Flagler. Rockefeller was working as a grain commission agent when he became acquainted with Flagler, a commission merchant with the Harkness Grain Company. By 1867, Rockefeller had left the grain business and started his own oil refinery. He approached Flagler in pursuit of capital for expansion of his venture and eventually made him a partner in exchange for $100,000 raised from Flagler's wife's cousin Stephen Harkness, one of the richest men in Ohio. This partnership would become the Standard Oil Company.

Rockefeller provided the spark that got the business started. Flagler, a great Integrator, devised a system of rebates to strengthen their position against competitors and with the transport providers. These rebates put

Standard Oil in a position to outcompete other oil refineries, and by 1872 nearly all of the refining companies in Cleveland had merged with Standard Oil; by 1880 it controlled the refining of 90% of the oil produced in the U.S. According to Edwin Lefevre in "Flagler and Florida" from *Everybody's Magazine* in 1910, "When John D. Rockefeller was asked if the Standard Oil Company was the result of his thinking, he answered, 'No, sir. I wish I'd had the brains to think of it. It was Henry M. Flagler.'"

Together, in their decades of working closely, Rockefeller and Flagler built the largest oil empire the U.S. has ever seen.

THE TWO COULDN'T BE MORE DIFFERENT

At this point, it should come as no surprise to you that Visionaries and Integrators, while complementary as a pair in the business, are quite different as individuals.

V/I Side-by-Side Comparison	
VISIONARIES	**INTEGRATORS**
Solve big complex problems	Identify and articulate the problems
Generate 20 new ideas per week	Make the best ideas a reality
Are great leaders	Are great managers
Are optimistic	Are realistic
Are "outside guys"	Are "inside guys"
Create the Vision	Execute the Vision

One V/I team with greatly contrasting individuals is Michael Morse and John Nachazel of the very successful Mike Morse Law Firm. It has grown by 50% per year for the last seven years. Michael hired John from outside the organization five years ago. Michael is a pure Visionary in every sense. He is the face of the company, a true celebrity in the marketplace, an incredible idea guy, amazing with the culture of the company and at inspiring the troops. John couldn't be more different. He prefers to remain behind the scenes. He is great at executing Michael's ideas. He loves numbers—forecasting, budgeting, and financial predictions—having dialed in every number in the firm as a science. John is truly the glue that holds the more than 100-person law firm together.

Michael and John are polar opposites. John's responsibilities and passions are to "analyze the data, identify and explain key revenue and cost drivers, manage people to help problem solve, drive continuous improvement, balance the workload, teach managers to manage by the numbers, and free up the Visionary to stay in his sweet spot."

Michael, in hearing John's list of roles, had a look of distaste on his face. He does appreciate the need for these responsibilities in his organization, but he's thrilled that he does not have to do them.

Michael's passions and responsibilities lie in the areas of new marketing ideas, growth ideas, inspiring the team, drawing the biggest and most impactful cases, shooting commercials, and doing his television show.

The extreme difference between these two individual's abilities creates an electric charge that continues to take the company to new heights.

THE TENSION THAT EXISTS

The polar differences between Visionaries and Integrators mean they are always driving each other a little bit
crazy. This is normal—just not easy. Imagine if their two
personalities were exactly alike. What gain would there
be for the organization? It would simply have more of the
same capacity. As with electricity, it's actually the degree
of difference (+/– polarity) that drives the opportunity for
an even greater charge. Polarity creates an electric charge.
In the case of a business, polarity energizes creative tension. When harnessed, this leads to a bigger impact. When
considering any problem, people who are similar will ask
similar questions. Our polarized V/I duo is likely to ask
very different questions—because they see the problem
from diverse vantage points. Varied lines of inquiry lead
to better results.

As Simon Sinek articulates in his excellent book *Leaders Eat Last: Why Some Teams Pull Together and Others
Don't*, "One point of view or a single, uncontested power
is rarely a good thing. Like the visionary and the operator
inside a company, Democrats and Republicans in Congress, the Soviets and Uncle Sam in geopolitics, even Mom
and Dad at home, the value of two opposing forces, the
tension of push and pull actually keeps things more stable.
It's all about balance."

Let's take a look at the intense V/I tension between
founding partners Scott Bade and James Leneschmidt
of ImageSoft. James and Scott have built their software
company from startup to $16 million in revenue. After
working together in their previous jobs, they took the

entrepreneurial leap together. They struggled during their initial growth stage because their completely different styles grated away on one another. They spent their early years co-running the company, not realizing that Scott was a Visionary and James was an Integrator. They had a hard time communicating and moving forward on what they wanted to accomplish. However, over time they started to appreciate their differences and better understand the value that each of their unique abilities brought to the company's success.

They have now firmly embraced their Visionary and Integrator roles—and the company is thriving. Of course, James's desire to have everything in place before taking a leap still drives Scott crazy. And Scott's desire to leap first and deal with the fallout later frustrates James. Yet no one can argue with their tremendous success in a very competitive industry. They've added 30 new people in just the last year. Their culture is the strongest it has ever been, and they have a rock-solid leadership team in place that is highly focused and accountable.

NOTHING LASTS FOREVER

As we're illustrating, it is not easy to work with your polar opposite—but the electricity can be powerful. You should also realize that forming a dynamic duo doesn't always work the first time. So what do you do if it flops? You simply try again.

One Visionary founder went through two Integrators before finding the right one. The first was a founding partner who never really carried his weight. This left the Visionary frustrated because he was always carrying a bulk of the Integrator load. Yet he procrastinated in making the tough change. After four years, the Visionary couldn't take it any longer and finally made the tough decision. He ended the relationship with his Integrator partner by buying him out.

Next, he quickly promoted someone from within the organization to become the next Integrator. This arrangement also lasted about four years. This time the Visionary himself was the problem. He never gave the new Integrator the autonomy to fully run the day-to-day affairs. That's largely because the person wasn't a true Integrator. This kept them from establishing the necessary level of trust. The relationship was destined for failure from the outset. Once again, the Visionary carried most of the weight until he ended the relationship.

Finally, he found the perfect yin to his yang. Not only did his new hire complement his unique style, this Integrator was tough enough to stand up to him. He had known the person in his industry for many years. They joined forces, and since that "marriage" four years ago, the company has grown 40% per year. The Visionary spends most of his time working on product creation, market research, company culture, and store development.

On the opposite end, we should note that even a great V/I combination doesn't always last forever. It moves through a cycle—which reflects both the growth of the business and of the two individuals involved. As the company's need for Visionary leadership evolves, so will that Visionary's need for the right Integrator complement. The two individuals may adapt in their evolving roles, right along with the business. Or they may not.

One of the great though little-known V/I pairs was Henry Ford and James Couzens of Ford Motor Company. Couzens was a co-founder and investor in 1903 when the company was formed, and in 1906 he became treasurer and general manager of the company. He had first proved himself as a great Integrator running Malcomson Coal Company. Its owner, Alexander Malcomson, was an early investor in Ford Motor Company, which was how Ford and Couzens met. That meeting was a match made in heaven.

Ford and Couzens were a textbook V/I duo. Henry Ford, as most of the world knows, was a true Visionary innovator who democratized the automobile, being fanatical about steadily lowering the cost of vehicles to make them affordable for everyone. While Ford is best known for perfecting the assembly line, he was also obsessed with making sure the vehicles were built right and serviced well. This led to every dealership having service departments.

Couzens exhibited all of the classic traits of an Integrator. Here is a description of him from the book *I Invented the Modern Age: The Rise of Henry Ford*, by author Richard Snow: "He got to his office in the Mack Avenue plant at seven in the morning and stayed there until eleven most nights. Everything that Ford couldn't do, he did. He took care of the books, of course, he kept a constant intimidating eye on the shop floor and he wrote lively and seductive advertising copy." He was the force behind the creation of the dealership network, and he remained fanatical about every detail. Snow's book further describes how Couzens strictly enforced the rule that every dealer have $20,000 worth of spare parts on hand, upholding the company's willingness to repair any Ford car no matter where it had been purchased. He ordered that at least one immaculate new model must be on hand at all times to show potential buyers. He also strongly suggested that if a disabled Ford had to be taken into the shop, the towing should take place after dark so as not to draw attention to the car's plight. Also, here's another little-known fact: Couzens, not Ford, instigated the raising of workers' pay to an unprecedented minimum of $5.00 a day, twice that of the industry average at the time. That generosity toward their labor force had a huge impact on the company's success in the early days.

A great quote in Snow's book affirms the power of this V/I duo. A descendant in the Ford family stated, "Ford by himself could not have managed a small grocery store, and Couzens could not have assembled a child's kiddie car. Yet together they built an organization that astounded the world." That idea is echoed in another observation, "Couzens . . . understood everything about the car business except how a car worked."

Unfortunately, this classic V/I marriage ended abruptly when Couzens resigned as general manager in 1915, and Ford bought all of Couzens's shares in 1919 for $29 million. Their relationship had begun to fracture in the latter years. They no longer saw eye-to-eye, and the tension present in any V/I partnership became sadly magnified to unmanageable proportions.

A Two-Piece Puzzle. Picture a two-piece puzzle that fits perfectly together along one edge. If the shape of that edge changes for one piece, the other will no longer fit—unless it also changes shape. If it can extend further in some areas and pull back in others, it may accommodate the new shape of its complement. Such adaptations might occur very naturally, or they may not happen at all.

The Visionary and Integrator are our two-piece puzzle, and the shape of their connecting edge is determined by their complementary degree of certain shared traits. It is important for you to understand that the shape of these two pieces is always moving over time. Sometimes the fit is nearly perfect; sometimes it is not. Often, it is somewhere in between. Consider the 12-year relationship between James Couzens and Henry Ford; the 7-year relationship of Bill Gates and Paul Allen at Microsoft. The fit changed over time, and the relationship eventually ended as a result.

Here is another example of a Visionary and Integrator that parted ways. The Visionary founder had, five years after startup, hired an Integrator who had previously worked for him in a different company. At first the relationship was a match made in heaven. At the time, the logistics company was generating $4 million in revenue. The duo enjoyed a great seven-year run together, more than doubling the size of the company to $8 million. Along the way the Integrator earned ownership as well.

Unfortunately, the business had also outgrown the abilities of the Integrator. The market had changed considerably, competition had increased, and the relationship became fractured during the final few years. Because each party felt the other was not living up to his end of the bargain, the Visionary terminated the Integrator and purchased his stock at market value. He now has a new Integrator in place. The new Integrator is better equipped to handle the new market dynamics and, frankly, is better able to kick the Visionary in the butt to stay 100% committed to the Visionary role. The company is now growing steadily to the next level.

THE VISIONARY SPECTRUM

It's important to know that not all Visionaries are created equal. Not every company needs a Steve Jobs. Not every Visionary is Walt Disney or Thomas Edison. Instead, each company's leadership takes a place along what we call the "Visionary Spectrum." The Visionary Spectrum assesses how much Visionary is needed in a particular organization. This determination changes based on three factors: (1) type of industry, (2) growth aspirations held by the leaders of the organization, and (3) the degree of change/complexity the company faces.

Let's consider each factor one at a time:

1. **Industry Type.** In the high-tech industry, a company needs a Visionary to be working, indeed, obsessing every minute of every day—because the industry changes so fast. As soon as you create a new product, it stands a good chance of becoming obsolete within months. On the other end of the spectrum, a property management company handling apartment buildings in the 1990s enjoyed a nice ride without needing much Visionary innovation. Of course, some property management companies in the '90s were extremely innovative, but many of them did not have to be.

2. **Growth Aspirations.** No matter what the industry is, companies have different growth trajectories. For instance, a company wanting only 5% annual growth is going to require a lot less Visionary innovation than one seeking 100% annual growth.

3. **Degree of Market Change/Complexity.** Given the industry and the time period, some organizations experience massive change and competition—and some don't. A company that needs to remain constantly on its toes will require a much more Visionary leader than companies in markets that are stagnant or below the radar of their competition and government.

Change/complexity can come from many directions: technology, pricing pressure, competition, labor markets, regulatory or environmental dynamics, and so on.

When you combine these three factors—type of industry, your desired growth rate, and the degree of complexity in your market—you will find where your company is on the "Visionary Spectrum." If all are redlined on the scale, then you might need Steve Jobs. If all are on the extreme low end of the scale, then Mr. Magoo might do. (For our younger readers, Mr. Magoo had very weak vision.)

Based on the type and amount of Visionary, you can then calibrate the need for a certain type of complementary Integrator. Walt Disney, one of the greatest Visionaries of all time, needed a very strong Integrator—like Roy. Yet if a Visionary is not spinning out new ideas in a flood, managing the business is a less complicated task.

For these reasons, no two V/I combinations are the same. Put another way, every Visionary isn't for every Integrator, and vice versa. One size doesn't fit all. Just like the two puzzle pieces, not all fit together. When they do fit together—it works. Some Integrators have Visionary traits that could complement a Visionary's weaknesses. Some Visionaries have Integrator traits that could complement an Integrator's weaknesses.

A great V/I combination from the 1950s and '60s is the successful combination of Soichiro Honda and Takeo Fujisawa of Honda Motor Company. Honda exhibited all the classic signs of a "flaming" Visionary, and numerous stories of taking risks and being innovative have been chronicled about him. He was quite a colorful character, reportedly throwing a geisha out of a second-story window, appearing inebriated during a vital presentation to bankers, and even hitting one worker over the head with a wrench.

He founded the company in 1948, recognizing Japan's post-war need for practical transportation. In 1946 he started out by purchasing 500 war surplus wireless radio generator engines and retrofitting them for bicycle use. When he ran out of engines, he began to develop and produce his own version. In 1949, as he was struggling through his first year, he partnered with Fujisawa. It was another match made in heaven. Fujisawa brought discipline to the company, along with funding and financial and marketing expertise. During their 25-year relationship, they rose to dominate the world motorcycle market. By 1974, motorcycle production had soared to 2,132,902 units, built by 18,455 employees.

Their relationship demonstrated a typical V/I dynamic. For instance, Honda created a breakthrough design that doubled the amount of horsepower generated by competitive four-stroke engines. Fuel was scarce and expensive; Fujisawa pushed Honda to produce an economical four-stroke engine. Honda decided to bet everything on the idea, and it was the turning point in the company's history. Its success allowed for new investment. There were some 200 other Japanese motorcycle manufacturers in the early '50s; they soon began to fall by the wayside. He also pursued a "shiny object"—our term for an advance of a Visionary that doesn't fit the company's Core Focus—that paid off when he ventured into international motorcycle racing. This led Honda to create more powerful engines and lighter bikes, which eventually triumphed in the commercial market against their competition.

Fujisawa was a good Integrator. He was the one who reined Honda in from his racing passion and pointed to the more "mundane" requirements of capitalizing on these innovations for racing and applying them to the commercial market. He also continued to shore up and strengthen operations by raising funds to invest in manufacturing resources. This enabled Honda to reduce dependency on suppliers and to set up its own distribution network, ultimately becoming a full-scale motorcycle manufacturer.

Through the many examples in this chapter, we hope you now realize the value of this dynamic duo. Still, the sad truth is that for most companies, their duo isn't so dynamic. Many duos are at their wits' end because the relationship is dysfunctional. Just as bad, many Visionaries don't have an Integrator at all, and many Integrators remain undiscovered by the right Visionary.

ARE YOU READY?

If you are a Visionary without an Integrator, how do you know when you are ready for one? We consistently see four factors that drive such readiness.

The Four Readiness Factors

1. Financial readiness (affordability)
2. Psychological readiness (ready to let go of some control)

3. Lifestyle readiness (ready for fewer hours, or the same hours with a different focus and less frustration)

4. Unique Ability® readiness (ready to be 100% you)

While appearing in no particular order, these readiness factors may evolve slowly over time until they reach some "tipping point." Sometimes, the shift from being without an Integrator to creating the V/I duo can be linked to a specific trigger—or triggers. Some are external, some are internal. These triggers seem to simultaneously impact one or more of the readiness factors above, accelerating the timeline for reaching that tipping point. The most common triggers we see are:

- Growth trajectory changes
- Self-awareness
- Frustration at "hitting the ceiling of complexity"
- Meeting their Integrator "match"
- Increased complexity in market conditions
- Various life events: kids, loss, marriage, etc.
- Loss of energy, or no longer wanting to continue the same pace

If you are ready, Part Two of this book will provide you with the essential How-To's for leveraging the value of a healthy V/I relationship. In the next four chapters we will give you everything you'll need for finding each other, clarifying your roles, and working together in a highly productive fashion. So, let's get to work.

PART TWO

THE HOW-TO'S

CHAPTER 4

THE ACCOUNTABILITY CHART

The truth is that everything up to this point was the easy part—helping you see how powerful the V/I relationship can be. We now move to the part that takes a little more effort—how to make the relationship productive.

As you know, making any relationship strong takes effort. What we will do is reduce managing your relationship to just a handful of practical disciplines. While they are simple, they are not always easy. However, if you will commit to applying them, they will give you a rich return on your time invested.

The first is a very important tool that will be the focus of this chapter: the Accountability Chart. The Accountability Chart will help to create a context for both your V/I relationship and your entire organization. When applied, it goes to the root of most of the issues you face in your V/I relationship. That is why it is the perfect place to start.

As Buckminster Fuller said, "If you want to teach people a new way of thinking, don't bother trying to teach them. Instead, give them a tool, the use of which will lead to new ways of thinking."

We want you to see your role as Visionary or Integrator according to where you fit in the Accountability Chart. It will feel restricting at first, and also rigid, but you will come to realize that it is not. All freedom comes from laying down boundaries. With an underpinning of structure, you will actually free up creativity and exceptional results. We have taught this tool to thousands of Visionaries and Integrators, and there is no denying its effectiveness.

THE ACCOUNTABILITY CHART

In order to lift your relationship and company to the next level, you must structure your organization—the *right* way. The Accountability Chart can create that *right* structure. This is a supercharged organizational chart. When completed, it will help both owners and leadership team members (mainly the Visionary and Integrator) clearly grasp their roles and responsibilities. That will, in turn, enable them to do the same for their people.

The essential first question is this: What is the right (simplest and best) structure to move your organization to the next level? What is the structure that will get you to where you want to go?

The Accountability Chart forces you to view your organization in a different way by being intentionally proactive about your structure, rather than reactively adapting a structure to fit your current people. When you see it in this light, you can address issues that have been holding you back.

For this tool to have impact on your company and relationships, you'll need to follow a few ground rules:

1. You must look forward. You cannot look back or get caught up in the present. It will distort your judgment. Focus on what you need, not what you have. Start as if building from scratch.

2. You must detach yourself from the existing business, your current role, your ego, and any emotionally charged thinking. Be open-minded.

3. You must elevate yourself above the business, looking down on it from that perspective, so you can make decisions for the greater long-term good of your company.

With these three ground rules embraced, the Accountability Chart stems from a fundamental belief that there are only three major functions in any business. Those three functions make every organization run, regardless of whether it's a startup business or a large corporation.

To illustrate the three major functions, picture three boxes side by side. In the box on the left, you have the first major function: Sales and Marketing. In the middle box is the second: Operations. In the box on the right, you have the third: Finance and Administration. You may call them by different names, but those are the three major functions of any company. Sales and Marketing generates business. Operations provides the service or manufactures the product and takes care of the customer. Finance and Administration manages the monies flowing in and out, as well as the infrastructure.

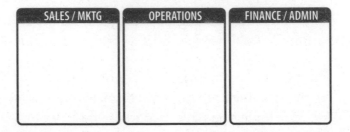

Assuming that these three major functions exist in all organizations, the next truth is that they must all be strong. If any of the three major functions are weak, your organization is not as effective. Strong means that each function is respected and understood in your organization, with a talented leader running that function like a well-oiled machine. It is also important that you believe that all major functions are equally important.

In order to maintain accountability, only one person can ultimately be in charge of any major function within your organization—and it must be transparent to all. Only one person oversees Sales and Marketing, only one person runs Operations, and only one person manages Finance and Administration. When more than one person is accountable, nobody is.

When leadership teams do this exercise for the first time, they often discover they have two (or even three) names in a single box (function). This may happen with you as well. If it does, you've uncovered one of the root issues for your company's lack of growth—or state of chaos.

You must solve the problem by reducing the number of names in each box down to one. The all-for-one-and-one-for-all approach won't build a solid company. It may have gotten you here, but only clear accountability will boost you to the next level.

To take structure a step further, we'll state that these three functions cannot operate independently of each other. That's where the Integrator comes into the picture.

As we've established, the Integrator is the person who harmoniously integrates the major functions of the business. When those major functions are strong, and you have strong people accountable for each, healthy tension will occur between them. The Integrator blends that friction into greater energy for the company as a whole. Said another way, the people heading up the major functions report to the Integrator. Therefore, the Integrator function is added above them in the Accountability Chart.

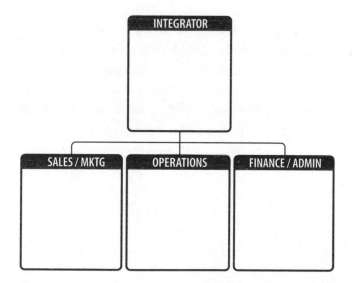

That is the basic structure of the Accountability Chart. With that understanding, two other important considerations need to be taken into account when creating the right structure for your organization.

No Two Accountability Charts Are the Same

First, recognize that no two companies' Accountability Charts are the same. You must customize it to suit your company's needs, size, growth trajectory, type, and direction, in order to create the *right* structure for advancing to the next level. When customizing the Accountability Chart for your company, the three major functions might split into more functions. For example, Sales and Marketing sometimes splits into a distinct Sales function and a distinct Marketing function. Operations sometimes splits into two or three distinct functions such as Delivery, Project Management, and Customer Service. Finance and Administration can split into as many as four: Finance, Administration, Information Technology (IT), and Human Resources (HR).

Depending on the size and state of your organization, you will end up with anywhere from three to seven major functions on that front line. As long as you stay focused on the essential first question of deciding what the *right* structure is for moving your organization forward, the right number will come. A note of caution: please remember that less is more. As leaders, you have an obligation to simplify your organization wherever you can. To that point, rarely do our clients end up with more than seven major functions. You can see in the example below that the hypothetical company has seven major functions: Marketing, Sales, Operations, Customer Service, IT, HR, and Finance.

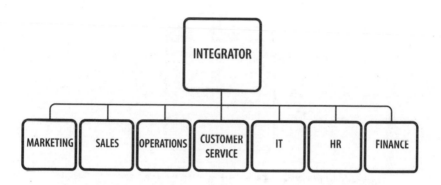

The Visionary

Second, the final element of your structure is the Visionary function. The Visionary shows up directly above the Integrator function. It is important to stress that the Integrator reports to the Visionary. That is why it is vital to illustrate it this way. As we move forward, you will see how structuring the relationship in this fashion increases effectiveness and solves many organizational problems.

For the sake of keeping things simple, we will move forward with a hypothetical company having three major functions: sales/marketing, operations, finance/admin.

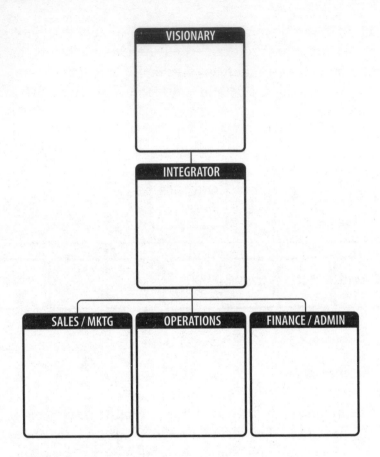

FIVE MAJOR ROLES

What makes the Accountability Chart more than just an organizational chart is that once the major functions are clear, you must then define the five major roles of each function.

The five major roles for the Visionary function are always customized for the individual who owns it. The Visionary, along with the team, must establish those five major roles based on how the Visionary can add the most value every day. This can be challenging, as team members may be reluctant to suggest anything to a company owner.

As an example, the Visionary function's five roles might be as follows (these are the most common):

- New ideas/R&D
- Creative problem solving
- Major external relationships
- Culture
- Selling big deals

The Integrator function's five roles might be as follows (these are the most common):

- Leading, Managing, and holding people Accountable (LMA)
- Executing the business plan/P&L results
- Integrating the other major functions
- Resolving cross-functional issues
- Communication across the organization

Establishing the five major roles for the other functions is normally pretty straightforward. The following

Accountability Chart shows the most common examples of the five major roles for each major function.

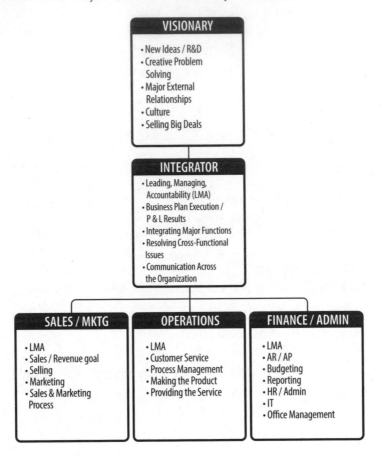

As noted in the illustration above, "LMA" stands for Leading, Managing, and holding people Accountable. Anyone in the Accountability Chart who has people reporting to him or her has a vital responsibility of LMA.

The following are quotes straight from the mouths of those performing Visionary and Integrator roles from a diverse cross-section of companies. We hope these will help you choose your five roles for your function in the Accountability Chart. These are their actual responses when asked what they do in their role.

As a Visionary, I . . .

- see things that aren't there or haven't been seen before.
- visualize all possible scenarios and identify the probable outcome.
- think sideways, live in the "what if" space.
- super-simplify complicated things to core elements, and toss the rest.
- drive strategic business development.
- open doors and influence key sales opportunities.
- come up with new products and enhancements.
- see the future possibilities.
- see the big picture and how all the pieces fit together.
- am the spark and energy for the culture.
- champion our Core Values and Core Focus.
- keep an open mind. Listen to the team.
- stretch others to think outside the box.
- generate ideas.
- sit on top of the ship and look out for icebergs.
- establish the common vision for where we are headed, and engage others in it.
- am the face of the organization.
- drive big deals.

- inspire others.
- create vision, direction, and the big picture.
- ensure brand consistency and growth.
- see and connect the dots.
- coach and mentor.
- provide a sounding board (safe zone) for the Integrator to bounce ideas and get honest feedback.

As an Integrator, I . . .

- am the "answerer" for functional leaders.
- act as a filter.
- prioritize.
- provide direction.
- keep the team focused on reaching our goals/completing our quarterly targets.
- move the team to action/get things done.
- help solve client and people issues.
- retain and grow great talent.
- keep everyone on the same page.
- convert vision to strategy to tactical plans.
- collaborate with the Visionary on his or her vision.
- provide a sounding board for the Visionary.
- help to determine when we need to stay focused and when we need to begin new initiatives.
- hold the leadership team accountable to the vision, goals, and quarterly targets.

- coach the team.
- make sure the organization has the proper structure, with the right people in the right seats.
- am the "man in the middle."
- manage the day-to-day, and integrate the major functions.
- execute the business plan.
- make the company profitable.
- get things unstuck and over the finish line.
- improve and maximize how the key functions work together.
- help everyone understand how they fit into the whole.
- remove obstacles and barriers.
- create harmony among the leaders/keep the peace.
- drive the tempo.
- structure the path forward.
- play devil's advocate for the Visionary.

As you construct your Accountability Chart, create only the right structure and roles first. Don't put any names in any of the boxes yet. Once you've illustrated the correct functions at all levels in the organization, add the five major roles to define what each function is accountable for—and only then add the accountable person's name. Once the function and roles are defined for your structure, we'll refer to each box containing a named function and its five major roles as a "seat"—building on Jim Collins's terminology of having the "right people on the bus, the wrong people off the bus, and the right people in the right seats." With the right structure in place, we will now move forward to putting the right people in the right seats.

When you choose someone to fill a seat, you want to be certain that person is operating in his or her God-given talent. When you're finished, the Accountability Chart should look like an organizational chart, with five bullets that illustrate the accountabilities of each major function and the name of the person in that function. This is illustrated in the following visual.

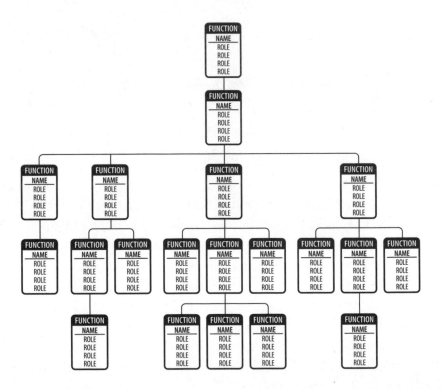

Important note: the Accountability Chart will clarify function, roles, reporting structure, and who's accountable—but it will not define communication structure. Your communication should flow freely across all lines and departments where necessary, creating an open and honest culture. With each position's accountability clear, and communication crossing all departments, you will avoid cross-departmental issues. The Accountability Chart should in no way create silos or divisions.

YOUR LEADERSHIP TEAM

With the completion of your Accountability Chart, the Visionary, Integrator, and the people heading up the major functions are your Leadership Team. When your Leadership Team is together, you now have representation and accountability for all the major functions of your business. The box in the following visual (with six major functions) shows your Leadership Team.

YOUR LEADERSHIP TEAM

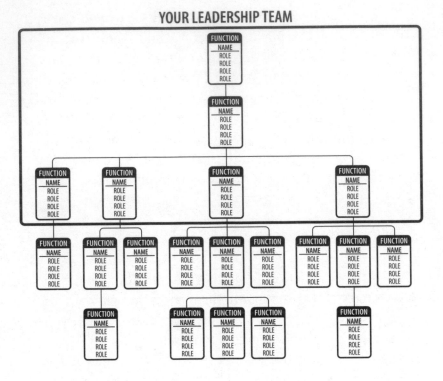

As Visionary, this should give you peace of mind that you will be fully connected to your leadership team and all the goings-on in the business. In the next chapter we'll discuss five "rules" that will help your team more effectively work together. And we'll discuss how to avoid the negative effects of meddling, tampering, and cutting your leaders off at the knees.

Before leaving the Accountability Chart, we should remind you that most of the companies we work with are privately held companies in the range of $2–$50 million with 10–250 people. That is our target market, where 80% of the companies we work with reside. Beyond that range, the Accountability Chart can begin to become much more complex.

THE TWO-PIECE PUZZLE

With your Accountability Chart now complete, we want to return the focus to the roles of the V/I combo.

Any given V/I pair may discover that they have some shared traits. This is okay. It's actually quite normal. Each individual will have varying degrees of Visionary strengths and weaknesses. Over time, some may have mastered their weaknesses to a certain extent. When this happens, they are no longer as magnified or extreme as they once were.

A Visionary, when considering a list of Integrator traits, may think, "I do that, and I'm pretty good at it!" While this may be true, the Visionary's true nature is still there—just beneath the surface. When honest with themselves, they will often admit that while they "can" do a particular Integrator task, they don't love doing it. At least not doing it consistently, every day, always. They are actually more inclined toward other traits, which align more closely with those on the Visionary list. When this happens, make the distinction clear by defining the roles correctly in the Accountability Chart. For example, some Integrators may carry the "Culture" role in their seat instead of the Visionary carrying that role.

Whether a Visionary or an Integrator, most individuals only bring about 80% of all the classic traits described in the previous chapters. The V/I relationship balances out to fill those other gaps that make up the remaining 20%. The best combinations will collectively give strong representation of all the traits needed most for a given business. Keep in mind that no two V/I combinations are exactly alike. Each will have its own unique signature. Think of two unique strands of DNA coming together to form the perfect double-helix. This is anything but cookie cutter. Sound challenging? We'll lay out a proven matching process in the chapters just ahead.

WE DON'T NEED NO STINKING TITLES!

If we had our way, we would eliminate the titles of CEO, president, COO, or general manager. We believe that you actually have a "Visionary" and an "Integrator" role. We encourage you to *internally* abolish those other traditional titles. They only lead to internal confusion about communication and accountability while contributing to political dynamics that are quite dangerous. If you need to show a traditional title on your *external* business card, to help you effectively deal with customers, vendors, shareholders, and the outside world—then do it. Just don't muddy up the waters inside your organization with titles that don't tell your people anything about what you are actually doing for the team and company.

COMMON ISSUES

With the Accountability Chart in place, most Visionaries and Integrators face four common issues that need to be smoked out and ultimately solved. Here they are:

1. Not Letting Go. The Visionary often wants to hang on to a particular seat or role (most commonly, the Finance seat or some of its roles) through a direct relationship. This is not necessary. With the right person in the Finance seat, the Visionary can let it go—trusting that the Integrator will hold them accountable. Also, with the formation of a true Leadership Team and the implementation of the Accountability Chart and the 5 Rules from the next chapter, the Visionary already *has* full communication with the head of Finance (and the rest of the Leadership Team, for that matter). They can talk all they want. It's just important for the Visionary to not *manage* the other functional leaders.

Similar desires for people to hang on to various areas they've previously held can lead to requests for "dotted line" relationships. These are not necessary either, and they add complexity and confusion to your structure. As we've discussed, accountability is most effective when it is a simple one-to-one relationship. This is your chance to obliterate all those confusing dotted lines! Remember, anyone can talk to anyone about anything.

2. Sitting in Multiple Seats. The second common issue is sitting in multiple seats. Earlier, we mentioned that only one person can command a major function. This does not mean that one person can't command two functions. In the early stages of a company's life, Visionaries and Integrators frequently sit in multiple seats. The Integrator often sits in the Operations Leader seat. Occasionally, a Visionary will also sit in the Sales Leader seat. This is fine as long as two conditions are met. First, the role should be consistent with their Unique Ability®— something they really want to do and are good at. Second, they will report to the Integrator in that specific function. In the usual reporting structure, the Integrator reports to the Visionary. Yet if the Visionary sits in a major function (often Sales or Marketing), they must report to the Integrator for that role. Otherwise, the Visionary can wield power that a typical Sales leader wouldn't have. That has the dysfunctional effect of cutting the Integrator off at the knees.

3. Wearing Multiple Hats. If a Visionary or Integrator is sitting in multiple seats, they must remember which hat they are wearing at any given time. The best way to illustrate what we mean is to use an example.

One client was a Visionary who sat in three seats, and therefore wore three hats. She was the co-owner of a $2 million technology company where she was Visionary, head of sales, and also managed the tech team. She was burnt out and overwhelmed, but she could not afford to hire people to fill those seats. She did have a partner who was a great Integrator, but unfortunately, he was just as overwhelmed.

Because she was wearing so many hats, she didn't know if she was coming or going. In an attempt to clarify where she was spending her time, and to help her to determine which role to hire for first, we had three hats made for her—with three titles on them: "Visionary," "Sales," and "Techs." This was fun, and she got a good laugh when she received them. While she didn't actually wear the hats, they created awareness. Most important, they helped clarify where she was spending her time and helped her to compartmentalize each function in her mind.

As a result, she was eventually able to hire a great manager for the Tech team. Now she wears only two hats—and has the capacity to do so. The company grew 20% last year.

Whether you are the Visionary or the Integrator, the point of this story is to always know what hat you are wearing whenever you sit in multiple seats. This will help you be honest with yourself, compartmentalize, and ultimately work to free yourself to have enough time and capacity to truly operate in your Unique Ability®—and get what you want out of your company.

4. Having to Sit in Both the Visionary *and* the Integrator Seats. It's common for an entrepreneurial company to initially have a Visionary alone—but no separate

Integrator. In effect, the Integrator seat is left empty. This causes a real struggle, because the Visionary is constantly frustrated with his lack of traction. In addition, he *has* to keep acting as the Integrator and filling that void, which repeatedly pulls him back into the day-to-day management of the business. In the beginning, this is a natural symptom of the evolutionary growth of the business. As the founding entrepreneur, he was the only one available to do these things—and they had to be done. As the business grows, this single combined V/I structure (and void) will tend to hang around for a handful of common reasons:

1. It simply hasn't occurred to the Visionary that someone can help run the company.

2. The Visionary can't yet see the financial payoff. Their conception of the benefit remains fuzzy, while the concrete costs of adding to the team are all too real.

3. The Visionary wants an Integrator and just can't figure out how to get one in place. Or even where to start.

4. The Visionary gets it (though they may not admit this to others) and simply doesn't want it. The idea of letting go, and giving up some control, doesn't sit well with them.

These four reasons explain why half the time, when we first engage with a company, we find a single combined V/I seat at the top of the Accountability Chart—occupied by a Visionary. For a Visionary to make the move from flying solo to a Visionary/Integrator duo requires her to be ready, willing, and able to allow a strong Integrator to be in place—so that she can fully assume the Visionary role for the organization.

It's vital that the Visionary gives the new Integrator room to operate—without meddling. A common problem in companies when a new Integrator joins is that the Visionary still tries to run the company. The two trip all over each other trying to co-run the company. In the world of the Accountability Chart, only one person can ultimately be accountable for a major function. This especially applies to the Integrator role. As we've already noted, when you have two people accountable, nobody is really accountable, and it leads to confusion and ineffectiveness.

DOES IT REALLY TAKE TWO?

The short answer is no. As mentioned earlier, half the time we find the Visionary and Integrator seats are both initially filled by the same person. On a select few occasions, the person sitting alone in both of these V/I seats is actually gifted with the rare capability of doing both. We see many people who *think* they are both—at least for a while. But they actually are not this rare individual we are about to describe.

We want to be very careful with recognizing this unique profile. We are concerned that many Visionaries will jump to a conclusion that they are this unusual character and not move forward to pursue a productive V/I relationship. You should not use this as an excuse for not taking the leap.

In our experience, this combined Unique Ability®
only happens about 5% of the time. One example is Todd
Sachse of Sachse Construction. Todd truly was this rare
V/I combination while running his company from $0 to
$100 million in revenue. He could have remained both the
Visionary and the Integrator if he hadn't set his sights on
growing the company to $500 million. Todd spent almost
20 years playing both roles and doing them well. However,
to grow the company five-fold over the coming years, he
recognized that he would not have the time to play both
roles well, and needed to divide and conquer by hiring
an Integrator.

Steve Barone of Creative Breakthrough Inc. (CBI), a
successful technology company, has a similar story. For
over 20 years he played both of the V/I roles very ably. If he
had decided that his $10 million company would steadily
grow from there, he could have continued wearing both
hats well. But after 20 years in business, he decided he
wanted to take advantage of market conditions and grow
his company to 20 times its current size. As a result, he
now plans to add an Integrator.

In both of these cases, you might say this story sounds
similar to that of many other Visionaries who hired Integrators somewhere along their journey. In fact, this is not
the case. Todd and Steve truly ran their companies well.
They provided high value in both roles—and could have
continued to do so. They truly possessed most of the traits
on both lists of V/I characteristics. Most other Visionaries
exhibit most of the characteristics on the Visionary traits
list and relatively few of the traits on the Integrator list.

So, as we leave this question of whether it really takes two, we ask you to be cautious. If you truly are one of those rare Visionaries that possess both sets of V/I skills, want to stay in both seats (combined) at the helm of your organization, and have the time to do so, that can work. We just ask that you are completely honest with yourself, as there is a 95% chance that you are not that rare person. Most of you will need a yin to match your yang as you build a great company.

With the Accountability Chart now firmly in place, we will address the 5 Rules for maximizing your V/I relationship.

CHAPTER 5

THE 5 RULES

You need absolute core alignment in your Visionary/ Integrator relationship to harness the power of the unique combination. Standing together is critical, as any small gaps between the two of you will show up as canyons to the rest of your team. One client, Jason Teshuba of Mango Languages, describes being totally in sync with his Integrator as "same pageness." You will achieve this "same pageness" once the Accountability Chart and the 5 Rules are firmly in place and being practiced.

On the subject of same pageness, Jason comments about his V/I relationship with Integrator Hamsa Daher, "It is absolutely essential for us to be on the same page. The knowledge that we are totally in sync gives me the comfort to let Hamsa run the day-to-day business operations. If I have the slightest suspicion that we are not on the same page, I start to meddle, and unconsciously communicate to employees that if you don't like Hamsa's decision, then you can come negotiate with me. This causes major problems in the long run, as it makes Hamsa feel disempowered and then causes me way more stress." He goes on to say, "I care about very high-level principles, and she cares about making practical day-to-day decisions. She is an awesome Core Values fit, so we can always let our values arbitrate any dispute."

If you really want to tap into the full power that your unique V/I combination can deliver, we urge you to adhere to the following 5 Rules. We will give fair warning: these are not easy and will require great discipline on your part. However, if a successful V/I relationship is what you want, the rewards for you and your company can be nothing short of astounding.

THE 5 RULES

1. Stay on the Same Page
2. No End Runs
3. The Integrator Is the Tie Breaker
4. You Are an Employee When Working "in" the Business
5. Maintain Mutual Respect

RULE #1: STAY ON THE SAME PAGE

A vital rule we've been teaching for many years is that the Visionary and Integrator must stay on the same page. This is accomplished through the Same Page Meeting. This makes the V/I duo, and ultimately the organization, much more effective. It eliminates dysfunctional, unproductive

Leadership Team meetings and interactions due to the lack of "same pageness" on the part of these key leaders. As an effective V/I duo, you really must be on the same page. If not, you'll either make your team uncomfortable or give them mixed messages.

The Same Page Meeting is a scheduled monthly meeting between only the Visionary and the Integrator. Allow two to four hours for the meeting, and always meet somewhere outside the office. Begin by "Checking In" with each other on a relationship level: How are you doing? What's your state of mind? What sort of business and personal stuff is on your mind? Remember, the V/I relationship is a sort of "marriage" within the business, so treat it like you would any other relationship of importance. Once you've both checked in, list all of your issues, concerns, ideas, and disconnects. Once you've built the full list, then identify, discuss, and solve (IDS) them (this is the Issues Solving Track we'll discuss next in Rule #3). You'll want to make sure you have allowed enough time to work through all the issues on your lists. Follow this agenda:

Same Page Agenda

- Check In (How are you doing? State of mind? Business and personal stuff?)
- Build Issues List (bring issues to the meeting)
- IDS (Identify, Discuss, and Solve issues)

The Same Page Meeting is an extremely effective way to help you air out issues, build and strengthen your relationship, and keep you in sync. That leads to your presenting a united front in the presence of your people, along with a consistent message that eliminates organizational confusion.

It is vital that you do not end the Same Page Meeting until you are 100% on the same page with each other.

RULE #2: NO END RUNS

At the heart of this rule is an attempt to obliterate situations where either the Visionary or the Integrator is doing things to impede the effectiveness of the other. They may feel very natural and harmless to you, but they can cause great damage.

An end run happens when an employee goes around a manager to complain or get a better/different answer to his problem. Unproductive complaining occurs when someone is sharing an issue not to solve it, but is instead politicking, backstabbing, and/or positioning. Every organization seems to have one person that everyone complains to, but if the person doesn't handle the situation properly, it can start the spread of a plague in your organization. The person being consulted in the end run can listen and coach, but never make a decision. When they do make a decision, they cut the manager in question off at the knees and leave her powerless to do the job she is there to do. Instead, they should listen carefully, and at the end of the conversation, ask "the question."

So, what's "the question" that you need to ask at the end of an end run, or after unproductive complaining? It's simply this: "Are you going to tell 'em, or am I going to tell 'em? Because one of us needs to tell 'em." We promise you that this works. This question will wipe out end runs organization-wide within a month.

Most end runs are taken to the Visionary. People in the organization are conditioned to go to the Visionary, or Visionary to employee, out of old habits. While this worked in the early stages of starting up and growing the company, you now have to implement Rule #2 to break these old, unproductive habits and grow to the next level.

RULE #3: THE INTEGRATOR IS THE TIE BREAKER

This rule addresses the fundamental questions about how decisions are actually made in the organization.

How do we know whose decision authority a given matter falls under? To answer this question, refer to your Accountability Chart. When it's well constructed, the roles associated with each seat in the Accountability Chart will guide you to identifying the proper owner of any given decision. The basic rule of thumb is that the Sales Leader owns decisions on Sales issues, the Operations Leader owns Operations issues, and so on. What we are addressing in Rule #3 is how issues pertaining to the company, Leadership Team, and day-to-day cross-departmental bottlenecks are handled.

We must start with the Issues Solving Track mentioned earlier. In the day-to-day operations of the business, and through the Leadership Team meetings, the Integrator will guide decision making through the Issues Solving Track outlined on the next page.

⊘ ISSUES SOLVING TRACK (IDS)

Imagine you and your V/I counterpart, along with your full Leadership Team, actually solving important issues in your regular meetings. Starting with your Issues List, identify the top three issues with regard to impact, and then follow the Issues Solving Track to move them toward a solution.

Step 1: Identify

- The stated problem is rarely the real issue.
- You have to dig down to find the real issue.
- Don't move forward until you clearly identify the real issue. Name it!
- The objective is to state the real issue in one sentence and hit the root.
- Once you have, then move to discuss and stay laser focused on the real issue until it is solved (no tangents).

Step 2: Discuss

- In an open and honest environment, everyone must share their thoughts, concerns, and solutions regarding the real issue.
- Discuss and debate.
- Everyone needs to get all they need to say out on the table, but only say it once. If you say it more than once, you are politicking.
- Once everything is on the table and the discussion is getting redundant, it's time for the solution.

Step 3: Solve

- With the greater good in mind, the solution is always simple, though sometimes not easy—and sometimes very hard.
- It's more important *that* you decide than it is *what* you decide . . . so decide!
- The solution needs to be stated by someone until you hear the sweet sound of agreement.

On a healthy team, eight out of ten times, everyone will agree with the solution. However, two out of ten times they won't, and the Integrator needs to make the final decision. Consensus management does not work. In fact, it will put you out of business faster than anything. Not everyone will be pleased in these situations, but as long as their views have been heard and the team is healthy, they can usually live with the decision. From there, the team must present a united front moving forward. It is okay to disagree with a decision, but once the decision has been made, everyone on the team must commit and go forward.

The thought of relinquishing this decision-making authority to an Integrator might be shocking or scary to some Visionaries. However, with the Accountability Chart and 5 Rules in place, our experience shows that it works. The ability to settle disputes allows the Integrator to execute by not letting the Leadership Team get stuck in holding patterns. A great Integrator will make better decisions than a Visionary because of being better in tune with all issues, priorities, and resources.

Should the Visionary ever trump a decision by the Integrator? The short answer is yes, although extremely rarely. If so, how? If an Integrator is making bad decisions, is not comfortable with certain decisions, or major decisions have to be made and he is not ready to make them, those decisions should get moved to the Same Page Meeting issues list.

With that said, if in fact the Integrator is uncomfortable and/or is consistently making bad decisions, he needs to be fired. Note: this should come as no surprise to either the Visionary or the Integrator, given the Accountability Chart and 5 Rules they've been living by.

Most of the time, big strategic decisions are covered in the Same Page Meeting. For example, large capital investments, changes from the agreed plan for strategic direction, and leadership-level personnel changes are all typically discussed there first.

RULE #4: YOU ARE AN EMPLOYEE WHEN WORKING "IN" THE BUSINESS

According to this rule, if you are a Visionary or an Integrator and also an Owner, you must recognize that your role as an "Owner" is different from your role as an Employee. A Visionary is usually an Owner, and about half the time we find that to be the case for an Integrator as well. Too often, a feeling of "owner's entitlement" carries over into the performance of their specific role in the Accountability Chart. As you would expect, this can create tremendous disruption in the organization. It creates fertile ground for the end runs we set out to banish in Rule #2, and nurtures the perception of a "Do as I say, not as I do" persona.

To address this tendency, you must understand that being an "Owner" *of* the business is different from being an "Employee" *for* the business. When sitting in the Owners Box (described below), you are playing your role as an Owner. As Owner, you benefit from your share of the profits generated by the company. You set the vision and strategy for the company and make the ultimate decisions. When sitting in your Visionary or Integrator seat in

the Accountability Chart, however, you must be accountable for your role and play by the same rules as everyone
else in a seat. Being an Owner sitting in an Accountability Chart seat should entitle you to no more rights
than an Employee sitting in an Accountability Chart seat.
You must keep these two roles separate. There is a time
and place for each of them. As in the story from Chapter 4, with someone wearing three different hats in their
Accountability Chart, you now have another hat: "Owner."

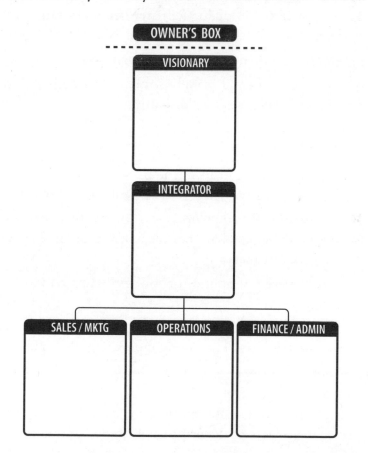

Here is a set of tenets to keep you out of the traps of Owner/Employee hat confusion and help you consistently live by Rule #4.

As Owners (only applicable for Partnerships):

1. Hold formal quarterly Owner meetings
2. Have monthly Same Page Meetings
3. Communicate in a straight line—no being vague
4. Engage in 50/50 dialogue, listen/let them talk, hear each other
5. Present a united front "in" the business
6. Solve issues before bringing them "in" the business; all company issues are fair game

As Employees:

1. Present a united front in the presence of others, and don't expect any special entitlements as an Owner
2. Integrator makes final decisions "in" the business, and any disagreements are handled in V/I Same Page or Owners Box meeting
3. Don't engage in politics or pull end runs with other people
4. Have complete accountability for the role/seat; play by the rules; you must be the right person in the right seat
5. You can be fired

Note that your only entitlement as an Owner is to receive your share of the profits distributed and to be the ultimate decision maker. Ownership does not carry with it any right to employment. If you are not the right person for the seat, you should be removed from that seat—for the greater good of the organization.

RULE #5: MAINTAIN MUTUAL RESPECT

As a dynamic V/I duo, you must truly respect each other. This cannot be faked, as your actions will be easily apparent to others in your organization. If you have a lack of respect for each other, you must end the relationship. Life is too short.

You must share a high level of trust, openness, and honesty as well. Anything else sends signals to the organization that will chip away at your ability to build a truly great company.

Regardless of equity interests, the Visionary should genuinely treat the Integrator as a partner—not as a minion. While the Integrator is accountable to the Visionary, he should not be made to feel "less than." A healthy, respectful relationship empowers the Integrator to go forth, practice, and maximize her craft—for the greater good. Equally important, this level of respect frees up the Visionary's creativity to do the same. It should be a relationship of mutual respect, built on trust—just like any good partnership or marriage.

This point about mutual respect can be exemplified by an actual epic session with one client, taking 16.5 hours to complete. (A typical session is a full day, with the entire leadership team, running about seven hours.)

This was the longest session ever, and clearly did not need to go that long. The reason for this protracted gathering was that the Visionary and the Integrator did not respect each other. As a result, that level of dysfunction consumed almost ten unnecessary hours. That time could have been applied to much higher and better use. Having to endure the countless hours of jabs and distrust also greatly hurt the Leadership Team's confidence and effectiveness. The happy ending of this story is that the Visionary ultimately parted ways with the Integrator (who was a partner) and now runs an incredibly successful, fast-growth technology company.

Simply put, you should never make a negative comment about your V/I counterpart to anyone in the organization—ever.

While the 5 Rules outlined above will go a long way toward building and maintaining mutual respect, in order to ultimately make your V/I relationship everything it can be requires constant discipline. There will always be some level of healthy tension; it's a matter of managing and harnessing it for the company's greater good.

FRICTION

Because a Visionary and Integrator are wired so differently, approaching the world in fundamentally different ways, natural friction is created between you. The stronger and purer the V/I roles, the greater this tension can become. This "charge," while a source of the V/I duo's power, can also become their Achilles' heel if not proactively managed. If the friction builds up for too long without being diffused, it can create a barrier that will keep the V/I duo from effectively addressing the core issues. Both Visionary and Integrator must constantly work to reduce this normal relationship dynamic. The 5 Rules create a never-ending process of managing this healthy friction.

You need to understand that tension is normal and should not be confused with any lack of respect. To combat and endure the friction actually demonstrates your high level of respect for each other.

Finally, be aware that some Visionaries initially respond to this new V/I relationship with a feeling of being "put out to pasture." This usually passes once they realize they are still very much connected, contributing, and communicating with the entire organization. The Visionary has numerous opportunities for ongoing inter-actions. Rather than being put out to pasture, you have been freed up to engage your true God-given abilities, and the organization is now drawing on your greatest talents.

Although it is rare, some Visionaries will engage in a regular cycle of one-to-one meetings with Leadership Team members, and perhaps even the Integrator, to feel even more connected. While this is fine, if the Account-ability Chart and 5 Rules are implemented, we find that Visionary one-to-ones are not necessary.

To summarize, we urge you to create an Accountabil-ity Chart as well as master and live each day by these 5 Rules. Leverage them together to create clarity, focus, and accountability for you and your entire organization. Do this and you will enjoy a healthy V/I relationship.

CHAPTER 6

FINDING EACH OTHER

If you have yet to find your V/I match, this chapter is about matchmaking: Visionaries finding the right Integrators, and Integrators finding the right Visionaries. As a Visionary, if you have decided that you are ready to bring on an Integrator, we will help you find the right match.

On the other side of the lens, while Integrators don't go out to hire their own Visionary, we do have some guidelines for Integrators "at large" and Integrators in the making, many of whom are currently tucked away somewhere inside large corporations or small companies. Please know that $2–$50 million companies really need you. We will show you how to find a great Visionary match and help them build a great company.

We have broken this chapter into two parts. Part 1 is for Visionaries seeking Integrators. Part 2 is for Integrators seeking Visionaries.

PART 1: VISIONARIES SEEKING INTEGRATORS

To keep things simple, we will start with a basic context. We have found that only three scenarios exist in companies that do not yet firmly have an Integrator in place:

1. You cannot identify an Integrator among the current team—you'll have to look outside.
2. There is an Integrator in your organization somewhere, but you just have not recognized them yet—and they are just waiting to be discovered.
3. You have an existing Visionary/Integrator combination (typically a partnership), but your two roles have not yet been clarified to divide and conquer.

We will address all three of these scenarios and provide practical solutions to help you find each other and ensure a great fit.

Integrators—A Scarce Commodity

Finding Integrators in the world of small businesses ($2–$50 million) is hard. One recruiter noted, "There's a gap in the world." According to one profiling expert, "Only about 22% of the world is even cut out to become a Visionary," yet the real problem pops up when he explains that only 5.5% of the world is truly cut out to be an Integrator. That leaves us with a daunting 4:1 ratio of Visionaries to Integrators. Now, if any Integrator could conceivably work with any Visionary, it would mean that if we engaged every Integrator, 75% of the Visionaries (3 of the 4) would still be left solo—with no Integrators remaining with which to pair. We know that the typical Visionary's competitive nature assures them that they would certainly be among the fortunate 25%—the ones that secured a V/I match. But the math gets worse.

The V/I match is like a carefully matched puzzle piece—no two are exactly the same. One Integrator does not fit the purposes of all Visionaries. In fact, if we assume that only 10% of all Integrators are the right match for a given Visionary, your odds of matching up fall from 25% down to 2.5%. Said another way, of all the Integrators out there, only 2.5% are likely to be a great match for you. That's scary!

But let's look at the figures another way. Out of every 300 million people, there are 16.5 million Integrators (5.5%). Of those, 1.65 million (10%) could be the perfect fit for you. So get moving! Go out there in the world and find a great match—before they pair up with some other Visionary.

To assist you in your search, here's our Proven Process for finding your perfect Integrator. The process for finding a great Integrator is actually not rocket science. It just takes time, commitment, and energy.

The V/I Connection Process—7 Steps

1. Use the Visionary Spectrum to determine how much Visionary your company needs
2. Map your Visionary profile

3. Identify your ideal Integrator profile—your complementary puzzle piece
4. Use the Four Readiness Factors to confirm that you are ready for an Integrator
5. Initiate your search and find your Integrator match
6. On-board your new Integrator and ramp-up
7. Follow the V/I Relationship Cycle—Plan, Execute, Same Page, Align

STEP 1—Use the Visionary Spectrum

Revisit the Visionary Spectrum (discussed in Chapter 3 on page 63) to validate where you are on it. This will help to create some perspective about what degree of Visionary your company really needs. Remember, the Visionary Spectrum is based on three factors:

1. Type of industry
2. Growth aspirations held by the leaders of the organization
3. The degree of change/complexity being faced by the company

Combine these three factors to get an idea where your company sits on the Visionary Spectrum. If all are redlined on the scale, then the company needs lots of Visionary energy. If most factors are on the extreme low end of the scale, then you only need a little.

Depending on where you fall on this spectrum, that will help you gain clarity on where you really need to spend your time. You will also develop better insight regarding what you will need most from your Integrator complement.

STEP 2—Map your Visionary profile

Once the Visionary Spectrum is clear, you'll need to document the pattern of how you most naturally operate—defining your puzzle piece in this two-piece puzzle. This will in turn dictate the profile of your ideal Integrator and the shape of the second puzzle piece for STEP 3.

As you work to understand exactly what your Visionary puzzle piece looks like, you should revisit the Visionary DNA discussed in Chapter 1 (page 22), along with the Visionary Indicator Assessment (page 24). Work through them carefully to calibrate a solid sense of your various strengths and weaknesses, and any gaps that will be particularly relevant for this V/I Connection Process.

Profiling tools and programs can also be extremely helpful in designing the two puzzle pieces. When Urban Acres's Visionary Steven Bailey decided it was time to find his Integrator, he engaged the assistance of Culture Index Dallas-Fort Worth—an expert firm in assessing, diagnosing, planning, and executing on all people decisions. They attack the problem from an inside-out perspective, working from the Visionary out instead of prospective candidate survey in. The program starts with the strategic direction laid down by the Visionary.

They worked with Steven's profile in conjunction with his personal "wish list" for the Integrator position. From this information, Culture Index Dallas-Fort Worth developed a map for Urban Acres's Integrator profile—a process that they call a "C-Job." Think of this as an objective for the benchmark ideal Integrator profile they hoped to find in their search. Armed with this intelligence, Steven targeted his search and then filtered all candidates by running them through the online candidate filter. In the end, Steven actually hired a candidate who very likely would not have been hired without the insight of the Culture Index program. As it turns out, some of the dimensions of his ideal Integrator combine to form a personality that doesn't always come across well in interviews. Because the team knew this going in, they were able to target their questions to explore the critical areas more deeply. Ultimately, they penetrated the candidate's rough exterior to reveal just the Integrator they were looking for—and he has proven to be an excellent complement for Steven.

In addition to the Culture Index program, we've also known clients to use DiSC, Kolbe, Myers-Briggs (MBTI), and TTI. If you are interested in such a profile-based approach, we encourage you to engage an expert to guide you. If you don't currently know of or have an expert, please visit our site (www.rocketfuelnow.com) for a current list of expert resources to help you with your V/I Connection Process.

STEP 3—Identify your ideal Integrator profile

Looking at the shape of your Visionary puzzle piece as defined in STEP 2, draw out its perfect complement. CJ Dube, an experienced Certified EOS Implementer, prescribes that her Visionary clients spend a scheduled two hours of quiet thinking time to create a "wish list" of what an Integrator would do for them. What freedoms, accountabilities, and responsibilities do they want? How could their life be different/better? How could their business be healthier and smarter? Once these questions are answered, incorporate these items into the design of your Integrator's seat.

Go back to the Integrator DNA (page 43) and Integrator Indicators Assessment (page 45) we discussed in Chapter 2 to help you create your profile and design your complementary puzzle piece. Work through them in comparison to your Visionary puzzle piece and map out the perfect match.

As mentioned in STEP 2, consider using a profiling expert for this step. We highly recommend it—as long as you are comfortable with the investment. Experts can consult with you on using powerful profiling technologies to help you identify the optimal Integrator puzzle piece to fit your Visionary puzzle piece.

If aggressive growth is a big part of your plan, you might want to consider looking for the next higher level of experience—toward what you want to become. Although this is not vital, and sometimes not possible, hiring an Integrator who has already worked at that level can be quite helpful in getting you there.

To save you time and cut to the chase in creating your ideal Integrator profile, we recommend the following job description as a starting point for an Integrator. We have distilled the Integrator traits into a cheat sheet to help you define the role for your own organization. This list stems from our efforts to help one company find an Integrator. To crystallize a universal profile, we undertook an exhaustive collaborative effort with a team of EOS Implementers along with Rob Fricker, also an independent Associate of TTI Success International, a premier assessment-based talent management solutions provider. Our work clarified the eight most common Roles and Accountabilities for an Integrator.

The Integrator Job Description

1. Faithfully executes the business plan, achieving or exceeding planned P&L objectives.
2. Leads, manages, and holds the leadership team accountable for achieving agreed-upon commitments.
3. Integrates all major operating functions of the business. Ensures everyone is rowing together in the same direction. Models the way, always working toward the greater good of the business.
4. Resolves issues effectively—seeing real problems, being comfortable with conflict, calling out the problems, and solving the problems in a practical and healthy manner. Ensures the leadership team is healthy, functional, and cohesive.

5. Ensures that everyone is truly following and adhering to the company's core processes and operating system with consistency. Demonstrates effective project management skills.

6. Dependably demonstrates a relentless obsession with values alignment, focus, simplicity, and clarity.

7. Effectively collaborates with the Visionary and stays on the same page. Maintains a high level of mutual respect with the Visionary. Realizes the unique contributions and ideas that the Visionary has, and possesses an ability to filter and translate those ideas into functional plans for the company.

8. Confirms that all key messages are properly and consistently cascaded across the organization. Inherently ensures that everyone is in the know. Verifies that a high level of effective communication exists throughout the organization.

Please use your creativity and experience as well in finalizing the right job description for your ideal Integrator.

STEP 4—Use the Four Readiness Factors

We don't want to fool you: choosing an Integrator entails hard work and takes time. As Dan Sullivan says, "There's either going to be long-term suffering, or short-term suffering. You choose. Either way there will be suffering." Before you begin this important search process, you must make sure you are ready to commit by reviewing the Four

Readiness Factors outlined in Chapter 4. To recap them, they are as follows:

1. Financial readiness (affordability)
2. Psychological readiness (ready to let go of some control)
3. Lifestyle readiness (ready for fewer hours)
4. Unique Ability® readiness (ready to be 100% you)

Do you see the financial benefits that will outweigh the expense? Are you really willing to let go? How attractive is the prospect of working fewer hours or spending those same hours squarely in your sweet spot? Are you ready to start being the you that only you can be? We urge you to confirm that you can deliver a resounding yes to these factors. If you can't fully commit, you will have false starts.

On the expense side, make sure you are ready for the investment. Realize that you'll need to pay your Integrator fairly. Based on our experience, most Visionaries initially underestimate what they'll need to pay their Integrator. So if you are a typical Visionary, take the Integrator compensation number you are thinking of right now and add 50% (the normal amount by which a Visionary will undershoot the right number). One great way to help you satisfy the financial readiness factor is to study your Issues List and note any issue that could be solved by adding the right Integrator. Now assign a financial impact to solving each of those issues—how much money and time would you save/make if each issue was resolved? Finally, total those amounts. How much is your number? If you are like most of our clients, that simple exercise makes a pretty clear case for the financial impact and return on investment your Integrator can bring.

STEP 5—Initiate a search and find your Integrator match

If you are ready, it's time to begin your search. Given our scarcity discussion at the beginning of this chapter, your first challenge will be finding enough candidates. One recruiter suggests that you'll want to consider 150 "qualified," 20 "interested," and 5–7 "highly qualified" candidates. Another reports 150 "leads" to identify 10 true "prospects" that convert to 3 "qualified" candidates. How will you find them? These are the six paths frequently taken by our clients.

1. Recruiters. Most Visionaries don't have enough people to appraise within their own network, and search firms can add substantial reach in your quest for candidates. Most search firms want to cull from 200–250 people, and finding that many is difficult. They have disciplined cold-calling processes that can be hard for a company to match on their own. Mike Frommelt from KeyStone Search, a firm that specializes in hiring Integrators, says that "generating an adequate pool of qualified candidates is far and away the biggest challenge of this process." If you aren't willing to do the extensive research required to source your pool of candidates, we recommend hiring a recruiter. Good ones are worth the investment. We urge you to have them read this book so they clearly understand the Integrator position you need filled. If you choose to explore this route, hopefully you already know a great recruiting firm. If not, ask around or visit our site (www.rocketfuelnow.com) for a current list of expert recruiters to help you with your search process.

2. Networking. This approach leverages your network via the reach you can get through one degree of separation. By putting the word out in your sphere of influence, good old-fashioned word of mouth can possibly bring the right potential candidates to your attention.

Michael Morse found his Integrator as a result of putting the word out. A business acquaintance, who happened to be his executive screener, knew a neighbor he believed was the ideal candidate. And they've proven to be one of the best V/I duos we've seen. This is also how Gino found his Integrator and business partner, Don Tinney, for EOS Worldwide. Gino put the word out to his sphere of influence, and a mutual friend connected the two of them. They recently celebrated eight years of a successful business partnership.

Networking means putting the word out to everyone in your network. One way is sending out a description of your desired complementary V/I puzzle piece via email, and you can also discuss your specifications in every conversation. Social networking platforms such as LinkedIn are also excellent channels to make your network aware of your search.

3. In-House Recruiting. If your HR department is strong and your in-house recruiting process is effective, it should provide you with great candidates. Have them follow this V/I Connection Process to focus their resources on finding the right Integrator for you.

4. Inside Candidate. Would someone on your current leadership team make the perfect Integrator for you? Is it a Partner? Don't forget to look inside—you might be pleasantly surprised by what you find. Once you create the target profile, run it on every person in your company.

5. Fractional. We have recently discovered that the "fractional" professional services model, already well known for finance and marketing roles, is beginning to expand to include the Integrator function. In this model, rather than bite off the full-time salary of an experienced hire, you engage that same level of resource (or sometimes even more experienced) for a less than full-time arrangement—perhaps three days per week. This can be a way to create immediate impact by adding the much-needed capabilities that you are currently missing while softening the financial blow of biting off the full-time hire all at once. This can be an option on an interim basis, and such a relationship can also evolve into a long-term full-time relationship.

We don't know of too many examples yet but have seen that it can work, and it seems to be becoming a popular trend. One example is Paul Boyd and his associates at Cloud9b2b. They have an expanding client base for this fractional Integrator service, and they have had a substantial impact in this role at Financial Gravity.

6. Additional Resources. We're here to help you get connected as well. Be sure to go to our website (www.rocketfuelnow.com) for a current listing of Integrators seeking Visionaries, and register yourself as a Visionary seeking an Integrator. While there, you'll also find our current collection of the most helpful additional resources we've found to assist you in completing your V/I Connection.

Whichever of these six pathways you choose, you will still need to be a masterful interviewer. If you are not, a good recruiter can also help fill this void. In the interview process, you are looking to assess three different dimensions:

1. How well do they fit with your Core Values? (They have to be a 100% cultural fit.)
2. How well do they align with your passion and purpose?
3. How well do they match with the roles and responsibilities you've identified for their seat in the Accountability Chart? Are you convinced that they *get* the role, truly *want* the role, and have the *capacity* to excel in the role?

Ask behavioral questions along these lines to get them talking. Describe your Core Values with passion, paint a vivid picture of your culture—and try to scare them away. If you can't scare them off, they're probably right for you. Listen to their stories. Probe for details and other examples. Take enough time to get comfortable with your assessment. Understand what they really want—and where their passions lie. We also recommend having some of your key Leadership Team members interview them. Are they a fit? Is the chemistry right?

As you broaden your candidate pool, and possibly begin pulling from larger companies, you'll need to communicate more about operational details that are less obvious to someone from a larger company. If they've not had prior experience in a 10–250-person company, there may be some things that they just don't "get" about small entrepreneurial companies. The pace is fast. Flexibility is essential. Everyone gets their hands dirty at some point. There are no "ivory towers." Walk them through the unique challenges of your environment. Then hit them with the unique opportunity that your entrepreneurial organization has to offer. They can have a bigger impact. More autonomy. An opportunity to grow toward mastery of their craft. Don't discount how rare those opportunities can be in large companies. Your world is someplace special—help them see that.

As the pool narrows to your final candidates, spend even more time with them. Group discussions. Dinner with other team members or even spouses. Meet the family. This is a crucial relationship, and you are essentially courting each other. And as with any courting, it is vital that there is chemistry in your relationship. Take as much time as you need to "date" before you decide to officially "tie the knot." We subscribe to the "slow to hire, quick to fire" philosophy, which means you should take your time hiring the right candidates. And if you do screw up (your gut will tell you if you did), quickly fire them and begin this step again. Making the wrong choice presents you with a great opportunity to sift through what worked, and what didn't, to help you hire better next time. Please don't confuse screwing up with the one year of patience we'll prescribe in the next chapter.

One client following this slow-hire, quick-fire philosophy hired a candidate who interviewed well and was extremely impressive during the hiring and on-boarding process. Within months, though, the client realized that they'd hired the wrong person and quickly terminated him. His comment regarding the candidate was that "he had great input but no output."

Compensation

When it comes to the question of an Integrator's salary, there is no one-size-fits-all solution. We wish we could give you one perfect answer—unfortunately, there isn't one. We see structures all across the board. Some with highly variable risk/reward, others mostly fixed. Some have a substantial equity linkage, while others have none. Just remember that most Visionaries underestimate the proper level of Integrator compensation. You must make sure that your compensation package is competitive.

Whether an Integrator comes from the inside or is hired from the outside, the Integrator may become an equity partner—but not necessarily so. We've seen no correlation between how successful an Integrator is and whether or not they received an equity stake. We find that about 50% do, 50% don't. Both work.

Once you've found the perfect fit, pop the question and exchange "I do's." Now it's time to make sure you do everything you can to get the partnership off on the right foot. That leads us to STEP 6.

STEP 6—On-board your new Integrator

Now that you finally have your Integrator in place, she seems to be a rock star. So let her run wild, right? Not exactly. The first 90 days of any leader's tenure will often make or break their success.

You'll want to pay close attention to two key milestones during the On-Boarding and Ramping-Up phase: 90 Days, and One Year. (We will focus here on the 90-Day On-Boarding, leaving the One-Year Ramp-Up to Chapter 7.) An experienced recruiter suggests you hire an onboarding coach for the first few months. On-boarding coaching has become very popular in the last few years. This coach will act as a sounding board for both you and the new Integrator and will ensure everyone is clear on what *success* looks like. This will add some expense to the overall process, but it is well worth the money. A quick Google search will find executive coaches in your area who specialize in on-boarding, and you can visit our website for additional expert coaches and on-boarding resources to help you. Also, the book *The First 90 Days: Critical Success Strategies for New Leaders at All Levels* by Michael Watkins is highly recommended as an additional supplement.

We urge you to take the first 90-Day milestone seriously. Do everything you can to make sure it is a meaningful checkpoint along the early part of your V/I journey together.

If you choose to manage your own on-boarding, make sure you take these five steps:

1. **Accelerate Learning.** Actively expose your Integrator to your most important stores of knowledge, whether they are other members of your team or the key elements of your information system. Actively coach your Integrator. Ask her questions to focus her thinking, and then teach her how to find her own answers.

2. **Secure Early Wins.** Nothing is likely to be more powerful in establishing a foundation for your Integrator, building her confidence, and positioning her favorably in the eyes of the team than some early wins. Help her find impactful projects that can be successful within those first 90 Days—then help her figure out how to make them happen. What a perfect context for learning and building a foundation for mutual respect.

3. **Achieve Alignment.** Go back to Chapters 4 and 5. Actively work through the Accountability Chart and 5 Rules together. Frankly, that process is the fastest way to achieve genuine alignment.

4. **Build the Team Dynamic.** Be sure to spend time helping your Integrator get to know the other members of the Leadership Team during those first 90 Days. Focus on helping establish a foundation of trust. Obviously, this will take time. In those early days, some unstructured social activities can go a long way toward integrating your Integrator into the Leadership Team.

5. **Provide the Tools.** Send your new Integrator to our website at www.rocketfuelnow.com for ongoing supportive tools, and have them read this book.

From here it is onward and upward. You might even get your life back! As you can see, the process of hiring the right person means committing to the work/details and not giving in to the temptations to take shortcuts. Your reward for doing so will be evident in 6–18 months when you are finally getting what you want from your business!

STEP 7—Follow the V/I Relationship Cycle: Plan, Execute, Same Page, Align, and Repeat

As with any great process, this one includes a feedback loop. Once your Integrator is On-Board and Ramped-Up, the journey begins. Apply the Accountability Chart and 5 Rules. You'll create a virtuous cycle of growth for the both of you, and for your business, for many years to come. Plan, execute those plans, stay on the same page, align as needed, and repeat.

PART 2: INTEGRATORS SEEKING VISIONARIES

Calling all Integrators!

Based on what you've read, are you an Integrator-at-Large? Are you living on the fringe inside a larger company? Feeling uncomfortable? Out of place, almost alien? Frustrated by how difficult it is to actually make things happen? Maybe you aren't working in a large company. Perhaps you are unemployed, or consider yourself unemployable? A recent college graduate? A consultant? Maybe you are even tucked away in a small company that hasn't realized what you could bring to their Visionary—the ability to harmoniously integrate all the major functions of their business. If so, you may be that special Integrator the small business world so desperately needs.

You may not be quite enough of a Visionary to have already set out on your own, yet enough of one to see how a successful company could work. You have that entrepreneurial curiosity that causes your colleagues to see you differently within a large organization. They aren't sure exactly what to do with you. Truth is, you probably scare them a bit, because they don't understand how your mind works. You seek more freedom. They are wired to be cogs in a machine. You are wired to take a vision—and go make it happen. That is a very special gift.

Visionaries need you to do just that. They are "stuck" without you—and need you to set them free. When you become part of a V/I duo, the Visionary gets exactly what they crave—the opportunity to move their vision forward. Steven Bailey, the Visionary of $3 million organic food supplier Urban Acres, says exactly that: "I get to keep moving forward. I get to keep dreaming big."

When you bring your Integrator talents into such a relationship with an equally talented Visionary, the payoff can be huge. Steven continues, "What's appealing to the Integrator is the realization that the Visionary is simply going to hand the vision off to him. The Integrator executes. It works. We both see the impact—and we get huge satisfaction from that."

Refer back to our Integrator Indicator Assessment in Chapter 2, page 45. If you exhibit these traits, please know that you have tremendous value—and a place in the world.

Likewise, if you know someone else that has these characteristics, let them know that they have a place in the world. Pass the word along. Hand them this book.

So how do we get you together with a Visionary? After reading this book, we hope that a good number of Visionaries will be looking for you. But don't wait for them—you need to be out looking for them as well.

We're here to help you get connected. Be sure to go to our website (www.rocketfuelnow.com) for a current listing of Visionaries seeking Integrators, and register yourself as an Integrator seeking a Visionary.

Look for business owners of $2–$50 million companies with 10–250 people. Use LinkedIn to do a search, and begin to build your "list" of companies where you might fit the bill as the Integrator for their Visionary. You might be pleasantly surprised by how many of these companies exist. Every major U.S. city has literally thousands.

Follow your local Business Journal or whatever publications tend to cover companies of this size. Strong Visionaries often draw a great deal of media attention— you will have a chance to read about them. Ask yourself if they sound like a Visionary that you would respect. Do you share their passion?

As your list begins to take shape, ask around. Put the word out in your network that you are interested in helping a Visionary entrepreneur make their vision a reality. Let everyone know this. Take people up on their offers to connect. Have coffee. Share your story. Share your passion. Explain how you see yourself impacting the life of that Visionary—and their company. If the person you are talking to is not that Visionary, boldly ask them to introduce you to others who are.

David Bitel of Randall Industries offers the following advice after having been the Integrator for two companies. When he found his present company, David says, "I'd been searching for a company that was experiencing growth. When I met Randy Pruitt, the Visionary of Randall Industries, his company was one of the few experiencing growth during an economic downturn." He added, "As we talked about the company's history of growth over the past few years, it became clear that Randy was filling both the Visionary and Integrator roles. He also mentioned that further growth was on the horizon and that he would have to make substantial investments in his company in order to manage the growth. He knew how and where to make these investments, but was concerned about how we would implement and manage them."

David went on, "It was clear to me that this was a Visionary in need of an Integrator to break through the ceiling." He added, "He was in need of the right Integrator to help him plan and execute his vision."

David humbly shares the following revelation about being an Integrator. "I don't think anyone ever sets a career goal to be an Integrator. That would be the equivalent of saying, when I grow up, I want to be the vice president of the United States, or I want to win a silver medal in the Olympics." He did admit, "During my career I realized that I lacked a few components of the Visionary DNA. However, I also came to realize that I can easily work alongside a Visionary, taking their passion and ability to see the sculpture in the raw granite and helping communicate that vision to the organization so we can make that dream a reality."

He offered the following advice for any Integrator seeking the right Visionary. "First and foremost, you must understand the type of Integrator you are. With that information, you must seek out the company and Visionary that best aligns with you. Second, you have to know if you are replacing a previous Integrator or filling the void for the first time for a Visionary. It's important to know this because you will need to learn very early what the Visionary is willing to let go of. A Visionary letting go for the first time is much more challenging than a Visionary replacing an existing Integrator. If you are good, however, your Visionary will eventually let go of everything they should."

When you do have an opportunity to connect directly with a Visionary, don't let them intimidate you. Visionaries typically look very confident on the surface and usually have very strong personalities. However, for all the reasons we've discussed in this book, you know they actually need help—and you should feel confident in approaching them.

Imagine asking them questions like these: What would it be like if you had someone you could trust to take your vision and make it happen? What if someone else could execute on all the little details so you could spend more time coming up with the next big idea? Would you like to be able to go away for an extended period and not worry that everything will come crashing down while you're gone? As an Integrator, you can be their answer to those questions. You clearly have an important place in the world. And the even better news is that you are outnumbered 4:1 by the Visionaries out there in need of you. You just have to find them.

CHAPTER 7

PATIENCE

We understand all too well the insanity in asking a Visionary to be patient. However, you need to understand what lies ahead when you join forces with an Integrator. A bumpy first year may well be in store for you. You have to take intentional steps toward being patient as you approach that initial difficult period. At times you may feel that you are pushing a giant boulder up a hill, and that it occasionally rolls back on you. Take heart! If you enter this process with your eyes wide open and bring disciplined focus to implementing the Accountability Chart and 5 Rules, you will survive the ramp-up stage. Unlike the mythical Sisyphus, condemned to push his boulder up a hill only to see it roll back down, over and over, for eternity, you will get your burden to the summit. Just lean into it and begin. This chapter covers the journey of creating a strong V/I relationship, and the patience required to develop that relationship. We will break this chapter into three parts: Before, During, and After the hiring.

BEFORE

You have seen that it takes time to find, recruit, and onboard the right Integrator. Be patient with your recruiting process. Resist the temptation to let your excitement and anticipation overcome your due diligence during the process. For such a major hire, you're better off slowing down in order to maximize your odds of making the right choice. Any prior experience you have of hiring quickly to drive production, with an expectation of acceptable churn, does not apply to hiring your Integrator. Take your time. Date a while before jumping into this marriage.

In the meantime, you must stay firmly engaged in the role of Integrator until you effectively install your new Integrator. Don't check out. Don't take your foot off the gas. You may be tempted to drop everything you've been doing as the de facto Integrator and rush off into your newfound freedom of playing 100% as the Visionary. Beware. You neglect the function of Integrator at your own peril. Despite the strong feelings that compelled you to begin the process of putting an Integrator in place, and any painful feelings they may include, just suck it up and keep doing it yourself until you have your new Integrator up and running.

Mark Bowlin was the first Integrator for Urban Acres. He explains the pattern for how their Visionary, Steven Bailey, would historically release control to someone on his team. "As soon as Steven gets the slightest inkling that somebody else has something, he takes his hands completely off the reins. And the reason that he doesn't feel like he can trust anyone is that his experience of when he has let something go like that—99% of the time—everything has fallen apart." He doesn't realize it's because he let go too soon.

You'll also want to proactively manage your existing Leadership Team and their expectations. Don't just steamroll them out of the blue with the news of a new Integrator. Spend some time preparing them for this change. For some of them the news of a new Integrator may come as a shock. Any move resulting in a new "boss" usually does. Present them with the value. Engage them in the conversation. Have them read this book. It should encourage you to know that many Leadership Teams really push to hire an Integrator. Once they understand the function, they instantly grasp that this will be the solution to a great number of their issues and frustrations. Show them the list of positive traits the new Integrator will bring. Get their buy-in.

Realize that this process may take a while, and know that it is worth the wait. Some clients have taken two years to find and align their V/I relationship to perform the way they want. Some others are still waiting . . . It simply takes time.

You should be aware that some Visionaries never do effectively make the transition. They undertake one or more false starts. Initially, they convince themselves that they want a change, and yet it never happens. A variety of behavioral patterns will undo your efforts to put an Integrator in place. You may encounter fear or resistance. You may be in denial about the impact of your own actions. You may be kidding yourself about what you are really willing to do to make the change happen. You might realize that you really just want to stay small, choosing to give up growth instead of letting go. Know this. If you are not ready, that is admirable to admit—there's nothing wrong with that. And being honest with yourself is clearly preferred to false starts. Some Visionaries aren't ready. Some will never be ready. Don't let this book force you to do something you are not ready to do—or that simply isn't right for you.

DURING

90-Day Milestone

As we discussed on page 127, an effective on-boarding process will maximize your odds of a successful integration. The first 90 days are critical, so make sure you have committed the resources necessary to build a strong foundation for your Integrator during that period.

One of our clients had their new Integrator spend their entire first 90 days just observing every aspect of the company. In weekly meetings, the new Integrator would sit quietly—for 13 straight weeks. On the 90th day, the Visionary turned the reins over to the Integrator. He found this modus operandi to be very effective.

The "listen first" approach is powerful for multiple reasons. Mainly, it helps the new Integrator understand the company's inner workings instead of immediately running the company while attempting to learn about everyone and everything simultaneously. The challenge for the Visionary is to be patient, being content to continue filling the Integrator role in the meantime. You'll also have to fight the feeling of not getting an immediately visible return on your investment.

Most Visionaries are too impatient to stick with this approach, but the Integrator will actually learn more about the company by just observing for a while instead of diving right in. We believe the Integrator should focus on asking more questions during the first 90 days versus jumping in with both feet.

One-Year Milestone

On average, expect a full year to elapse before your V/I relationship really hits full stride. This is a natural Ramping-Up period. You're both getting to know each other, firmly instituting the Accountability Chart and 5 Rules. Take the time necessary to let your alliance evolve into a healthy, high-functioning relationship.

One of the most effective V/I relationships is that of Michael Morse and John Nachazel at the Mike Morse Law Firm. Together they have tripled the firm's size and grown it to the largest of their specialty in their home state. Michael had been able to build his firm to an impressive size on his own, but realized getting to the next level would require an Integrator. In an interview with us, the duo shared some of the things they do to make the relationship work. First, they followed the "wish list" strategy. Michael listed every idea, worry, priority, and issue on his mind. These were all things he expected to be solved as a result of adding an Integrator. Michael explained, "John and I worked from that list every day for the first year." That list no longer exists, as fully implementing the Accountability Chart and 5 Rules has helped the two of them accomplish everything on it.

Michael Morse's Actual Integrator Wish List

1   Be the quarterback for the move back to Southfield, including phones, computers, boxes, furniture.

2   Review Insurance policies. Meet with agents. Compare prices and companies and coverages: workers compensation, business, home, lake house, malpractice, employee liability policy.

3   Help analyze and help implement east side office if it is a go.

4   Analyze numbers for each person. Help put a number on each person. Help us set proper goals for the coming year.

5   Set up and implement employee review system. Make sure it gets done and done right.

6   Help us come up with better bonus and compensation systems.

7   Go through and review all employee files to make sure they all have proper documentation signed and in file. Make sure all attorneys have signed contracts. Make sure they cover everything.

8   Get a handle on how we close files. Want to do it all on disk and get rid of storage costs. Get a handle on what storage company has and when we can start purging old documents to save money. Possibly purge half of what we have there, as we pay per box.

9   Make sure phones are being answered quickly and promptly. If not, figure out why.

10 Make sure all Core Values are being lived by all. Brainstorm and set up ways for the Core Values to become part of everyone's daily lives at the firm.

11 Make sure all 90-Day Priorities are being done and help people who are having a hard time getting them done.

12 Be my eyes on the books so I don't have to. Review bank statements. Watch money in account daily or weekly.

13 Review vendor list and start getting a handle on all payables and start negotiating and looking for alternatives. Example: copy services, postage, subpoena services, running/filing services, etc.

14 Review and perfect new employee time procedure.

15 Get a handle on what could make secretaries more efficient and happier.

16 Make sure everyone is working to capacity, no slackers.

17 Make sure office is as paperless as possible.

18 Interview and compare several Time Matters people and hire new person in office. Get Time Matters working as to make us more efficient.

19 Organize Word system so it's easy. Probably will need different software for that purpose.

20 Make sure clients are being called and informed about their pending cases. Follow up on it. Pull files and see if this is being done. Make sure lawyers are putting proper notes in files.

21 Get a good handle on lawyer teams and make sure they're running smoothly. Get a handle on capacity of each person.

22 Help us cut costs.

23 Come up with, manage, organize quarterly events for team building.

24 Review and negotiate all contracts, including advertising.

25 Look for missed opportunities for getting new business. Review what is and is not working.

(Continued on next page)

26	Be my eyes and ears when I am not there or when the rest of executive team is not there.
27	Be in charge of all scorecards, blue sheets, and gathering financial information. Interact with our lawyers and CPAs when needed.
28	Eventually run our quarterly meetings.
29	Make sure we roll out what and when we need to roll out.
30	Interview and make sure tech people and web people are the best we can get for the money.
31	Monitor what other employees are doing on their systems via monitoring software that has been bought and implemented.
32	Manage each team. Go to each team meeting. Make sure of good follow-through. Make sure team meetings and the team itself run smoothly.

Michael admits, "In the first year, I had my doubts. Frankly, I was convinced it wasn't going to work. I was frustrated, disappointed, mad, and disheartened. Things weren't moving fast enough. All of a sudden, at exactly the one-year mark, I realized and actually said to myself quietly—he's actually good at this." Michael continued, "It was hard to wait a year. I didn't want to." He went on to advise any Visionary looking for an Integrator that "nobody is going to be perfect, so don't fall into the trap of thinking that perfection exists. You'll drive yourself crazy."

Michael also offered up the following wisdom from his experience. "You must be completely open and honest with each other, have complete trust. Tell each other when you are not happy about something immediately—don't wait." He also recommended "talking every day" and "letting the relationship evolve."

An important factor that surprises many Visionaries is that a good Integrator does not need to know your industry. Michael's Integrator, John, knew nothing about the legal industry. Most of the time a great Integrator can learn the industry. Remember that James Couzens of Ford Motor Company knew nothing about how an automobile worked. Being a great Integrator depends more on the ability to manage human energy than being an industry expert.

The Visionary may also experience a phenomenon we call "Visionary Remorse." After letting go of some tasks they may have held for a long time, sometimes a Visionary feels they have been put out to pasture. That first year will likely bring turbulence—and your new position will certainly feel different for you. You may feel that you've lost a part of your identity and simply aren't contributing at the same level you have for years. This is clearly not the case. You should rationally know that you are now in a position to contribute at an even higher level—in a way for which you are uniquely suited. That said, you may still have such feelings. This "trough" usually lasts for 6–12 months. A great piece of advice from John Pollock, another Visionary client, is "Don't mistake activity for productivity. Creativity is productivity—it just doesn't feel like it at first."

The term "put out to pasture" is actually a direct quote from one Visionary who struggled with the clarity of his V/I relationship in the first year. He was the sole owner of his company. Once he put an Integrator in place, their roles were not clear early on. The Visionary used to enjoy being able to tinker with any aspect of the company whenever he felt like it. The reality was that his meddling was incredibly frustrating for everyone else in the company, a 50-person organization, especially the Integrator. Not surprisingly, the company hadn't grown in years. Upon clarifying the V/I roles, they really started to gain traction.

Unfortunately, even with momentum finally starting to happen, the Visionary was still reeling a bit. After a year, however, the Visionary clearly understood his real value. He then began applying his creativity to take the company international and create revolutionary new products.

AFTER

The "After" really has two parts. The first comes after you have ramped up your V/I relationship in the first year and it is working well for what are hopefully many years to come. The second part is when it doesn't work. Let's take them one at a time.

First: When It Works. Assuming you made it to the One-Year Milestone, and things are working, just keep living by the Accountability Chart and 5 Rules. That will lead you naturally through the ongoing V/I Relationship Cycle of Plan, Execute, Same Page, Align—and Repeat.

Dave Richards, Integrator for ROSSETTI, describes the relationship with his Visionary Matt Rossetti as follows: "Communicating with one another has been a journey. We inherently see things differently. We come at most issues from different places, but we have begun to embrace those differences and appreciate how our different points of view help bring us to a better place. We are getting better at communication. For some time in the past, we would discuss something, each expressing a different point of view, and we would each walk away convinced of the other's point of view while doing the opposite of what we each expected of the other. We can still struggle with our communications when we are both moving at the speed of light on projects, when we don't slow down enough to ensure a good exchange of dialogue and clarity of the point being made. The transition to a trusting partnership has been gradual and productive."

As we've mentioned several times earlier, another one of the best duos we've seen, now in the sixth year of their relationship, is Randy Pruitt and Dave Bitel. Together they have taken Randall Industries from $8.5 million to $20 million and are still growing. In an interview, they offered some insight for other V/I duos.

Dave, as Integrator, said, "What makes the relationship work so well is that we collaborate on Randy's vision. It could be a particular issue we need to solve, a new product to develop, or a new potential acquisition. Once the vision is clearly established, I create a strategy and next steps. These usually become our 90-Day Priorities." Dave also explains that to be an effective Integrator, you have to maintain a proper balance between the "in the business" and the "on the business" stuff. He says he accomplishes this by following the Accountability Chart and 5 Rules.

Dave says one of the greatest challenges an Integrator faces is managing the Visionary's expectations. He says that Visionaries have a certain DNA to dream of "what's next," and once they lock on to a new idea, they want to work quickly to accomplish it. These new ideas require a certain amount of change for the organization, and the Integrator needs to set the proper expectations for the Visionary, assuring him that the vision will be executed, but the timing may be longer than the Visionary desires.

Randy offered some equally helpful insight about the V/I dynamic. He describes his top three Visionary roles as: (1) Passion, (2) Industry knowledge, and (3) Leadership. He admits that in focusing a majority of his time on these three roles, his challenges are staying on track and focused, staying organized, and keeping his hands out of the details of the business. He says, "That is what Dave helps me do. He takes the projects and implements them, relieving my time to focus 'on' the business instead of 'in.' He allows me to not get distracted with daily operations. Without him, I'd have more stress and less time to work on company growth."

Randy goes on to offer the following advice, "If you are looking to grow your company, you can't do it without an Integrator. At some point you will have to relieve the weight carried on your shoulders and find someone to carry it with you."

Second: When It Doesn't Work. Unfortunately, the second part of After is: "What if the V/I relationship doesn't work out?" Sometimes it won't. Our passionate plea to you is this: If it doesn't work the first time, try, try again! Glean every lesson you can from the experience. Deeply consider what worked and what didn't. Conduct a postmortem autopsy on every component of the experience and treat it as a learning opportunity. Sometimes the Visionary is the reason the Integrator failed. Be open to seeing this, and don't let your ego keep you from learning that valuable lesson. Then get back up, dust yourself off, and—armed with the wisdom of your firsthand experience—get back to the business of creating the V/I relationship you want.

We've had several clients whose first attempt did not work. One came to the sad realization that his V/I duo was not so dynamic. At exactly the One Year mark, he decided it wasn't going to work. Reflecting back, he feels he couldn't have made the decision any sooner—and certainly couldn't wait any longer. His Integrator actually was somewhat effective, adding some value. What was brought to the table just wasn't enough to make financial sense, so he made the tough call. He had a very honest conversation, delivering the tough news. The meeting was so healthy that they were able to put in place an amicable transition plan for both parties.

The Visionary went on to conduct a full autopsy and inventory of the specific lessons learned from the experience. He used these lessons to do a better job of finding the right person for the role going forward.

CONCLUSION

That is our prescription to help you maximize your V/I relationship. Like many changes that are worthwhile, the path is simple—yet it is not easy. Based on our experience with thousands of companies, though, it works.

We love entrepreneurs. We love Visionaries and Integrators. You are our tribe, and our life's work is devoted to helping you get what you want from your business. We sincerely believe that the V/I duo is one of the most powerful discoveries for taking a company to greatness. We invite you to join our V/I community at www.rocket-fuelnow.com for ongoing teachings, insights, and stories to help you continuously take your V/I relationship to the next level. We are here to help.

BONUS CHAPTER

Out of respect to our Visionaries' attention span, this book is now complete. You've gotten all you need to have a great V/I relationship. If, however, you still have an appetite for a little more, the next chapter is a BONUS chapter. It is truly the "icing on the cake." The following BONUS chapter includes four of the foundational tools we teach all of our EOS clients. If you'd like a few more tools to get even more out of your V/I relationship, and your company, then please read on. On the other hand, if you are an EOS client or have read *Traction* or *Get a Grip*, then the following chapter might offer you a timely review of those tools.

THE ICING ON THE CAKE—5 TOOLS

FOUR MORE TOOLS

There are hundreds of management and leadership tools available to business owners who want to improve their business. As a Visionary, you've probably pursued dozens of them with mixed results. With the Accountability Chart you learned in Chapter 4, and the four additional tools in this chapter, there are a total of 5 Tools we offer you in this book. These five simple tools have the highest impact and require the least amount of time, so we encourage you to learn and master them. They have proven to effectively lay the foundation for a healthy V/I relationship and company. Master them, and you will experience a powerful charge of focused energy in your organization.

The 5 Tools

1. The Accountability Chart (covered in Chapter 4)
2. The Core Questions

3. The 90-Day World

4. The Weekly Level 10 Meeting

5. The Scorecard

That's it. Just 5 Tools. Embrace them and you'll have a rock-solid V/I relationship and well-run company. Let's take them one at a time.

TOOL #1: THE ACCOUNTABILITY CHART

The Accountability Chart, as you already learned in Chapter 4 (page 71), clearly defines the best organizational structure for your company. It also crystallizes roles, responsibilities, and reporting structure to help make your vision a reality. With clear accountability in place, you can now solidify that vision by applying the next tool.

TOOL #2: THE CORE QUESTIONS

Tool #2, the Core Questions, is a discipline to get you and your V/I counterpart both 100% on the same page with a clear vision and plan for your company. In order for you to make good decisions, you must be clear on your direction. To find the right direction, you must answer the Core Questions that follow. When you clearly know who you are, what you are, and where you want to go as an organization, you'll have an internal compass to guide you through the rough tides you'll undoubtedly encounter along the way.

In addition to having this internal compass to guide you, you will also avoid 80% of the potential symptomatic "disconnects" that occur by not being 100% on the same page with each other. While it is vital that you and your V/I counterpart are on the same page with the following questions (that is priority one), we strongly recommend that you engage your full Leadership Team in answering the following questions as well. This will create more buy-in from the team and produce an even better quality of work.

Question 1: What are your Core Values?

Core Values define who you are as a person, your culture, your guiding principles, and the rites of passage into your organization. When you know what matters most to you, the rudder on the ship you're sailing is much easier to control. You stay on course with less effort required, and you sail forward. This question is also vital to answer because if you do not have Core Value alignment between you and your V/I counterpart, it is a deal killer. The relationship will never fully blossom. You'll constantly be at odds.

You aren't just making a decision about your relationship, however. When your Core Values are clear, all of your people decisions will become simple. When people in your organization don't share your Core Values, they shouldn't be in your company.

If you haven't yet defined your Core Values and aren't sure of where to start, use the following list to stimulate your thinking. Then create three to seven that you feel define who you and your organization truly are (not what you want to be). A good rule of thumb is to think about your three best people and the characteristics that make them great. Between the characteristics you identify in that thought exercise, and those listed on the following list of examples, you should discover your 3–7 Core Values.

- Competitive
- Does the right thing—even when it hurts
- Compassionate
- Hungry for achievement
- Encourages individual ability and creativity
- Accountability
- Services the customer above all else
- Strives for perfection/Never satisfied
- Strives for continuous self-improvement
- Helps first
- Growth-oriented
- Mutually respectful
- Bases opportunity on merit, no entitlement
- Creative and imaginative
- Not cynical
- Humbly confident
- Gritty

- Self-propelled
- Hungry to learn
- Fearless
- Finds a way to say yes
- Walks the talk

Once you've discovered the Core Values that define you, bring them to life in your V/I relationship. Communicate them regularly and use them to evaluate everyone in your company. Make sure each member of your team is living by them and making every decision with these Core Values in mind.

Question 2: What is your Core Focus?

Core Focus is your company's sweet spot. Where do you excel? What do you love doing? What are you great at doing? What are you passionate about? Why does your organization exist? If you and your organization know the answer to this key question, it becomes a filtering and guiding mechanism for you to make decisions. For instance, if you decide that your sweet spot is in health and wellness, and someone approaches you to take your technology into an application for oil exploration, you have the foundation to make a very simple decision. RUN!

Crystallizing your Core Focus will create clarity to help you make good decisions. You'll be amazed by how it can reinvigorate you and your company. When you have this clarity and begin to align all of your people, processes, and systems with your Core Focus, you'll truly be operating in the zone, doing what you love and what you're great at doing. As a result, you'll see things more clearly and know what does fit—or what you shouldn't be doing.

This level of focus will give the Integrator clarity on where to aim all of the company's resources and maximize every opportunity. It will also keep the Visionary from getting distracted by "shiny stuff"—anything that is not in your Core Focus.

Question 3: What is your 10-Year Target?

10-Year Target defines the number one overriding long-range goal for your company. As Yogi Berra said, "You've got to be careful if you don't know where you are going, because you might not get there." Many V/I combos we work with have trouble thinking ten years out. That's a real obstacle to making better decisions.

If the Visionary wants the company to be four times its size in ten years, and the Integrator wants to maintain the current size, you have your answer as to why you're not making good decisions together: you're not on the same page.

When one client clarified its 10-Year Target, the two V/I partners realized they had two completely different goals. One wanted rapid growth, and the other was content. They decided to end the partnership, split the company, and worked out a separation agreement. The partner that wanted growth brought in a new Integrator. The following year, his company generated their highest revenue and the largest profit ever.

It is vital that you both create and agree on a one-sentence, long-range goal (five or more years out; most clients choose 10 years) that is specific, measurable, and attainable. Once you're clear on your longer-range target, you'll start making better decisions in alignment with that target.

Question 4: Who is your ideal customer, and what is the most appealing message to them?

In business, trying to do everything for every potential customer or client is a formula for organizational suicide. You can't be all things to all people. You don't need them all. You shouldn't want them all. You should decide exactly what you're selling in a short, sweet, and simple message and decide who your ideal customer is for that product or service. You'll clear the fog of whom you should (and shouldn't) be doing business with. That will in turn create a laser focus on who you should be targeting.

This level of clarity enables the Integrator to harmoniously orchestrate all resources and the Visionary to put all of his creative energy into a deeper, richer, understanding of your customer and your unique value proposition, therefore maximizing results. The two of you will make better decisions about marketing, selling, training, and hiring to attract and retain your ideal clients.

Question 5: What is your Three-Year Picture?

This is a vivid picture of what your company will look like in three short years. If a Visionary and Integrator can clearly see the same picture, and everyone's energy is going in that direction, you'll eliminate at least 50% of the confusion, murkiness, delays, and bad decisions that most teams experience.

Since most business needs are shifting so fast in the twenty-first century, there's little value in a highly detailed strategic plan, especially one beyond a three-year window. A lot can change during that time span. It is valuable, however, to create a picture of the future organization three years out.

This will accomplish two vital objectives. First, your V/I relationship will become 100% in sync because the plan will force you to push through and clarify any disagreements. Second, you will be able to share your vision with your people in a way that they will understand. Then they can determine if they share it, buy into it, and want to be a part of that vision. As Napoleon Hill said, "Whatever the mind of a man can conceive and believe, it can surely achieve." Once everyone sees the Three-Year Picture, you can make decisions to get there faster than if you didn't have a Three-Year Picture at all.

To create your Three-Year Picture, review your answers to Core Questions 1–4. Then select a date three years in the future. We recommend tying the plan to the end of a calendar year, making it easier to envision.

Next, determine the revenue for this time frame. Start with this question: What is the annual revenue going to be three years from now? This is always fun, because you find out if you are in sync about how fast you want to grow. You will typically set a range, but you'll have to settle at one number. More often than not, the Visionary will have higher goals than the Integrator. One new client's range was between $20 million and $100 million. At one end was the Visionary, and at the other end was the Integrator. Can you imagine how different those individual future views must have been? They can't co-exist in the same company without creating confusion and frustration. Eventually, they both got on the same page with a figure of $30 million.

Your Three-Year Picture should fit on one page, consist of 2–4 measurables at the top (e.g., revenue, profit, margin, a key measurable), and include 5–15 descriptive bullet points that clearly paint the picture (e.g., big breakthroughs, key marketplace victories, number of people, new offices, new marketing products, added resources, technology, process improvements). The reason for the bullet points is that they really help you uncover and clarify any disconnects. If you decided on $10 million in revenue, one of you might be thinking of 100 clients at $100,000 in revenue each, and your V/I counterpart might be thinking of 1,000 clients at $10,000 in revenue each. While both total the same $10 million of revenue, those two business models are very different in terms of how you build the infrastructure, what size prospects you should be targeting, and who you should be hiring. Now is the time to decide what it looks like so that you can start making those decisions. These details should be included in your Three-Year Picture.

Question 6: What is your One-Year Plan?

Next, we'll bring your long-range vision down to the ground and make it real. That means deciding on what you must accomplish this year.

Remember, less is always more. Most companies make the mistake of trying to accomplish too many objectives per year. By trying to do everything all at once, they end up accomplishing very little and feeling frustrated. When everything is important, nothing is important. This approach forces you to focus on a few goals rather than many. By doing that, you will actually accomplish more. That is the power of focus—it creates traction.

To create your One-Year Plan, decide on the future date. We recommend you sync up your date with either the calendar year or your fiscal year, regardless of where you are in the current year. So, if it's July, set your future date as December 31. After that, you'll set a brand-new full One-Year Plan each year. Having a partial-year plan in the first year simply allows you to gain some experience with the process between now and then.

As you did with the Three-Year Picture, again, decide on the numbers. What is your annual revenue goal? What is your profit goal? What is the measurable? This number should be consistent with your Three-Year Picture measurable.

With the Three-Year Picture in mind, discuss and decide on the three to seven most important priorities that must be completed this year in order for you to be on track for your Three-Year Picture. These become your goals. They need to be specific, measurable, and attainable.

Leave no wiggle room. An outsider should be able to read it and know what it means.

"Attainable" means that it's doable. Setting unrealistic goals is the biggest trap entrepreneurs fall into. You must believe it's possible to hit the goal, or else you can't hold each other accountable to it. If every goal is a "stretch goal," how will you know what success is? Goals are set to be achieved.

Your One-Year Plan should fit on one page, consist of two to four measurables at the top (e.g., revenue, profit, margin, a key measurable), and include three to seven goals for the year (hopefully, closer to three).

With your One-Year Plan now clear, you've answered the last of the Core Questions.

To summarize this tool, answering the Core Questions will lay the foundation to simplify your decision making. You'll have the clarity, the direction, and a guiding mechanism to make efficient decisions as a dynamic V/I duo.

With your vision now clear, take a second look at the Accountability Chart you created in Chapter 4. You and your V/I counterpart should be in total agreement and believe there is 100% alignment between your vision and your structure. Once that is the case, we can move forward with Tools #3–5.

TOOL #3: THE 90-DAY WORLD

The first two tools laid the foundation. These last three will help you gain tremendous traction to ultimately accomplish your vision. At the same time you'll keep your

V/I relationship strong and in sync as you work together in day-to-day execution. With a clear vision and structure in place, you're ready to establish short-term priorities.

The reason for the 90-Day World is primarily because 90 days is about as long as humans can focus an intense commitment to one thing. As a result, three months is the perfect increment to reconvene and reassess priorities. The other reason is that working relationships start to fray about every 90 days. That is the perfect time to get back together—just as things are starting to feel chaotic and people are starting to get out of sync. Sixty days is too soon, and 120 days is too long—hence the 90-Day World. There are four "90-Day" quarters in a year, and you can meet to set quarterly priorities.

One session participant illustrated the power of setting short-term priorities. Back in the days when his family picked cotton by hand, they would stand at the foot of the field, look out at the acres and acres of cotton, and feel overwhelmed by the work that needed to be done. To make the prospect of picking all those acres less daunting, a leader of the group picked up a stick and threw it as far as he could and said, "Let's just make it to the stick." Then everybody put their heads down and "picked to the stick." When they arrived there, they picked up that same stick, threw it out again, and repeated the process.

That's the same concept as the 90-Day World. Rather than be overwhelmed by the monumental task of accomplishing your Three-Year Picture or 10-Year Target, this 90-Day view enables you to break the longer-range targets down into bite-size chunks and focus on making it to the stick (the end of the quarter).

In the 90-Day World, you must establish only the three to seven most important priorities for the company, the ones that must be done in the next 90 days. You can call these priorities in the 90-Day World anything you'd like—objectives, initiatives, priorities. We prefer the term "Rocks," made popular by Verne Harnish, who borrowed it from Stephen R. Covey's time-management illustration in his book *First Things First*.

Covey illustrates the concept as follows. Picture a cylindrical glass container set on a table. Next to the container are placed rocks, gravel, sand, and a glass of water. Imagine the glass container as representing all of the time you have in a day (or "quarter," for the sake of this tool). The rocks are your most important priorities, the gravel represents your day-to-day responsibilities, the sand represents interruptions, and the water is everything else that you get hit with during your workday. If you, as most people do, pour the water in first, the sand in second, the gravel in third, and the rocks last, what happens? Those big priorities won't fit inside the glass container. That's your typical day. You'll never get the important stuff done.

What happens if you do the reverse? Work on the big stuff first: Put the rocks in. Next come the day-to-day responsibilities: Add the gravel. Now dump in the sand, all those interruptions. Finally, pour the water in. Everything fits in the glass container perfectly; everything fits in your day perfectly, and the important stuff gets done every quarter. The bottom line is that you need to work on the biggest priorities—the Rocks (90-Day Priorities)—first. Everything else will fall into place.

Once your vision is clear, you will set better 90-Day Priorities. Setting these Priorities becomes more simple. To establish your 90-Day Priorities, you must meet every 90 days. Not only should you have 90-Day Priorities, but each member of your Leadership Team should have 90-Day Priorities as well. The reason to limit 90-Day Priorities to three to seven is that you're going to break the habit of trying to focus on everything at once. It simply can't be done. By limiting priorities, you can focus on what is most important. Remember the old saying: When everything is important, nothing is important. With the increased intensity of focusing on a limited number, you will do better work and accomplish more. In the words of Dan Wallace, a Certified EOS Implementer, "Do less better."

The way you move your company forward is one 90-day period at a time, setting 90-Day Priorities that create a short-term focus. To the degree that you focus everyone in one direction, you'll gain the power and focus of a laser beam and gain faster traction toward your goals.

TOOL #4: WEEKLY LEVEL 10 MEETING

With the Weekly Level 10 Meeting, you will achieve a communication discipline we refer to as "keeping the circles connected." Imagine two rings side by side, not unlike the large steel rings that magicians somehow amazingly link and unlink in that popular illusion. Each ring represents one party in your V/I duo. The objective is to keep you two connected without letting you get too far apart (disconnected) or having you overlap too much—which produces a smothering effect. By keeping the circles connected in a V/I relationship, you stay in sync and eliminate potential relationship issues that can occur when the circles are disconnected. Said another way, when the circles are disconnected between two people, something bad is going to happen. Not because either party is bad, just because "out of sight is out of mind."

The Weekly Level 10 Meeting is a bulletproof, world-class weekly meeting that we teach to every client. The concept is currently being followed by thousands of companies. As we've already addressed, Visionaries can have a difficult time letting go of certain duties. Mastering this tool enables a Visionary to let go while still feeling fully connected to their V/I counterpart, the Leadership Team, and the organization.

This discipline continues the process of taking your vision down to the ground. We are now narrowing in from quarterly (90-Day) to weekly. Implementing this weekly meeting will create instant traction, keep your V/I relationship strong, and help you execute the vision. Once the quarterly priorities are set, you must meet on a weekly basis to stay focused, solve issues, and communicate. The Weekly Level 10 Meeting is your opportunity to make sure that everything is on track. If you're on track for the week, then you're on track for the quarter, and if you're on track for the quarter, then you're on track for the year, and so on. The Weekly Level 10 Meeting, like a heartbeat, creates a consistent flow that keeps the company healthy. Put another way, the Weekly Level 10 Meeting creates a consistent cadence that keeps you and your team in step.

Always a Level 10 Meeting

How would you rate your internal meetings on a scale from 1 to 10? When we've asked that question of thousands of leaders, the response is almost always somewhere between 4 and 5. That is not good enough. Most meetings in business are weak and not productive, and yours may be as well. By implementing the discipline of the Level 10 Meeting, you will raise that rating to a 10. The Level 10 Meeting Agenda is designed to keep your V/I relationship and leadership team focused on what's most important on a weekly basis. Nothing is more important than keeping your numbers on track, your 90-Day Priorities on track, and your customers and employees happy. The Level 10 Meeting is the most effective and efficient way to accomplish that.

A Weekly Level 10 Meeting keeps you focused on what really needs to get done, helps you spot developing problems, and then drives you to solve them. What makes for great meetings is solving problems. Patrick Lencioni says it best: "Your meetings should be passionate, intense, exhausting, and never boring." The Weekly Level 10 Meeting was developed because a number of clients wanted to know how to improve their meetings. It was created in the real world. The guiding principles are based on human nature.

The Weekly Level 10 Meeting

- Who: Visionary, Integrator, and full Leadership Team
- Where: The office conference room

- Duration: 90 minutes
- Frequency: Every week
- Prework: 90-Day Priorities established and captured on a one-page document; Scorecard filled in; Issues Solving Track (IDS—Identify, Discuss, Solve) understood by everyone

The Weekly Level 10 Meeting Agenda

- Segue (Good News)   (5 minutes)
- Scorecard   (5 minutes)
- 90-Day Priority review   (5 minutes)
- Customer/Employee Headlines   (5 minutes)
- To-Do List   (5 minutes)
- IDS (Issues List)   (60 minutes)
- Conclude   (5 minutes)

Two roles are vital in the Weekly Level 10 Meeting. One person must run the meeting (typically the Integrator). This person will move the team through the agenda and keep them on track. Second, someone must manage the agenda. This person makes sure that the agenda, Scorecard, and 90-Day Priorities documents are in front of everyone in each meeting. They update the To-Do List and Issues Lists in the agenda each week.

The meeting starts promptly. Football coach Vince Lombardi was famous for his mantra that early is on time, and on time is late. Arrive a few minutes early so you can begin to get your head in the game. The only reasons for missing the Weekly Level 10 Meeting are vacation or death. Even if someone cannot make the meeting, the show must go on. Don't reschedule it and don't cancel it.

The Weekly Level 10 Meeting Agenda

- Segue (Good News)   (5 minutes)
- Scorecard   (5 minutes)
- 90-Day Priority review   (5 minutes)
- Customer/Employee Headlines   (5 minutes)
- To-Do List   (5 minutes)
  - _____
  - _____
  - _____
  - _____
  - _____
- IDS (Issues List)   (60 minutes)
  - _____
  - _____
  - _____
  - _____
  - _____
- Conclude   (5 minutes)
  - Recap To-Dos
  - Cascading Messages
  - Rating 1–10

Everyone should have a copy of the agenda placed in front of him. Your To-Do List and your IDS Issues List should be included in the actual printed agenda (see visual above). It is a dynamic document where new To-Dos and Issues are added and subtracted each week. Your agenda should fit on one sheet so that you're only managing one piece of paper. You no longer need to take meeting minutes. They should be a relic of the past. If you want to know what was covered in a meeting, check that week's agenda.

Segue. The first phase of the meeting should set the stage to have a great meeting. As a team, you each share good news (both personal and professional). You are creating a transition from working "in" the business all week to working "on" the business, disconnecting from day-to-day affairs. Keep all electronic devices off the conference table so you can disconnect, take a deep breath, change gears, and connect on a human level. In addition, the segue brings a human element to the meeting and increases team health. For example, one leader might share, "My 87-year-old father was able to spend some time with us over this last week. It was so fun to watch the kids interact with him. He loves to hear about all the stuff they're into—and they just can't seem to get enough of his stories." Personal material like that reminds you that you are all human beings in this world trying to create something great. This agenda item should take no more than five minutes.

The next phase of the meeting is focused on "Reporting and Issue-spotting." Three segments are covered during this phase: Scorecard, 90-Day Priorities, and Customer/Employee Headlines.

Scorecard. The Scorecard (which we will help you create next in Tool #5 on page 176) review is an opportunity for the Visionary, Integrator, and full Leadership Teams to examine the 5–15 most important activity-based numbers in the organization at a high level and to make sure they are all on track for the week. Any numbers that are not on track are "dropped down" to the IDS portion of the meeting, which is your Issues List. Avoid any discussion here. The reporting phase of the meeting should merely identify problem areas. The biggest pitfall with most teams is that they reflexively launch right into discussing and trying to solve any issue uncovered during the reporting segment. You must fight that urge and be disciplined. That keeps the meeting on track. You will have plenty of time to discuss and solve issues during the IDS agenda segment, and the process will be much more productive when you're addressing all of the issues at once— in order of priority. Scorecard review should take no more than five minutes.

90-Day Priority Review. Next, you focus on your 90-Day Priorities to make sure that they are on track. Review each one at a time. Each person reports that his Priority is either "on track" or "off track." No discussion— the discussion will happen later. When a Priority is off track, it's dropped to the IDS portion of the agenda. "On track" simply means that the owner of the Priority feels she will accomplish it by the end of the quarter. Even if a Priority is on track but someone wants an update or doubts it is on track, it should be dropped to the IDS segment. The 90-Day Priority review should take no more than five minutes.

Customer/Employee Headlines. You share short and sweet headlines about any customer or employee news or issues for the week, either good or bad. For example, "Joe, our best client, is happy with the job we did last week," or "Darla is upset with the decision on the new benefits program." Any customer or employee good news is a time to pat yourself on the back. Any issues, bad news, or concerns that need further discussion should be dropped to the IDS portion of the agenda to be solved. Some companies have a formal customer and/or employee feedback system. If your organization does, this is when you would discuss those types of issues. Customer/Employee Headlines should take no more than five minutes.

After we complete the Reporting phase, we move into an Accountability phase—closing the loop on our commitments from the prior week's meeting.

To-Do List. At this point, you review all To-Dos from last week's meeting. From this review comes accountability. By incorporating this agenda item, you will accomplish more as a team. A To-Do is a seven-day action item. To-Dos are the commitments people made in last week's meeting. For example, "I'll call the printer tomorrow," "I will have it shipped this week," or "I will have every prospect on the list contacted by Friday." Quickly review each item on the To-Do List from a standpoint of "done" or "not done." If the To-Do is done, strike it from the list. If it's not done, leave it on the list. Rule of thumb: 90% of To-Dos should be "done" every week. Anything less is a sign that you have an accountability problem.

After moving quickly through the Reporting and Accountability phases, we are ready to move into the

"Problem-Solving" phase, where you should expect to spend most of your time each week. Solving problems.

IDS (Identify, Discuss, Solve). This is where the magic happens. It's time to tackle your Issues List. Great meetings happen when problems are solved. At this point, you should have 60 of your 90 minutes left for solving issues. This part should always take up most of your meeting. On average, about three to five issues on the list will be carried over from last week's meeting because they did not get solved. Additional issues are added on the fly, during the reporting phase in your review of the Scorecard, 90-Day Priorities, Customer/Employee Headlines, and To-Do List. On average, about 5 to 10 new ones are added each week. Typically, the new Issues List contains roughly 5 to 15 issues.

Although your Issues List is in your agenda, you can also write your Issues List on a whiteboard or flip chart in the meeting room. This puts it clearly in front of everyone. Many clients have said that this approach leads to even better participation and focus instead of everyone looking down at the Issues listed on their individual copies of the agenda.

You begin tackling issues by deciding which of the issues are the number one, two, and three in order of importance. Start with only the top three most important because, as a rule of thumb, you don't know how many you'll resolve, and you should never just start at the top of the list. Sometimes the most important issue is near the bottom. As long as you take them in order of priority, you're attacking the right ones. In addition, when you solve the most important issue, you tend to find out some of the other issues on the Issues List were merely symptoms of that core issue, and they drop off automatically.

Start with number one, and hash it out until it's solved following the Issues Solving Track: Identify, Discuss, Solve (IDS for short, covered in Chapter 5 in Rule #3). Then go to issue number two, and then number three, and then re-prioritize the remaining open issues. In some meetings you may only get through one issue. In others you might get through ten. You never know, but again, as long as you're taking them ranked by priority, you're tackling the team's issues in the right order.

Once the issue has been identified, discussed, and solved, the solution usually turns into an action item that ends up on the To-Do List. You may end up with one, two, or three To-Dos as a result of solving that one issue. In next week's meeting, you will confirm that those To-Dos were actually accomplished and that the problem has been solved forever. Otherwise, teams have a tendency to let issues linger for days, weeks, and even months as a result of not confirming that the agreed-upon action was accomplished.

Following the Issues Solving Track keeps a team focused on what's important, and it avoids spending time on what some may feel is a priority—but really isn't. This vital portion of the meeting should be passionate, intense, exhausting, and never boring. No one should engage in politics for a cause; the discussion should be open and honest, with everyone fighting for the greater good (the company vision). By solving all of your key issues for the week, you feel a tremendous sense of resolve and accomplishment.

Conclude. With five minutes left, move to conclude the meeting. This is your opportunity to pull everything together. You will frame everything that was discussed and make sure no loose ends are left.

Concluding has three parts:

First, recap your new To-Do List. Quickly restate all of the action items on the list to confirm they are correct, that everyone has theirs written down, and that they will be done in seven days. This step reinforces accountability.

Second, discuss whether any messages need to be communicated to the organization based on decisions you made today. Agree on who is going to communicate them, when, and what medium will be used. This step will greatly reduce communication issues that you may have encountered in the past, such as people being surprised by changes that were made without their knowledge.

Third, to help you get instant feedback on how you're doing, have everyone rate the meeting at the end on a scale of 1 to 10—with 10 being best. The minimum standard is to average an 8 or better—quickly progressing toward a 10 (thus the name Level 10). Rating the meeting will give you the opportunity to self-correct, because you will ask the team to explain whenever any ratings are lower than an 8. The end of the meeting should feel like the conclusion.

The meeting ends on time. This avoids any domino effect where meetings run over, pushing other appointments back and blowing up people's schedules.

The Five Points of the Weekly Level 10 Meeting

A productive Weekly Level 10 Meeting should meet the following five criteria. The meetings must:

1. Be on the same day each week
2. Be at the same time each week
3. Have the same printed agenda
4. Start on time
5. End on time

Scheduling the meeting at the same time every week creates a routine that is easier for everyone to plan around. Using the same agenda discourages reinventing the wheel; once you have an agenda that works, stick to it. Plus, it helps to keep the meetings consistent. Start on time, because when you start the meeting late, the part of the meeting that always suffers is the issues-solving time, and that's what matters most in the meeting. And end on time so that you don't push back any following meetings.

Be patient with the Weekly Level 10 Meeting. Your first few will be awkward, but as you stay committed to it, it will become very comfortable. The level of team health, communication, and results will consistently rise.

By setting 90-Day Priorities and implementing the Weekly Level 10 Meeting, you create both a 90-Day World and a weekly focus. You keep the circles connected between the Visionary, the Integrator, and the Leadership Team. You gain tremendous traction toward your vision. You are now doing what the successful V/I duos do. Your past frustrations start to subside, and you make progress on your way to helping your company and relationship evolve from chaotic to a well-oiled machine.

TOOL #5: THE SCORECARD

The final tool in your V/I toolbox is the Scorecard. This is how the Integrator remains accountable and how the Visionary keeps a finger on the pulse of the firm. This powerful tool enables both of you to truly let go and focus on the things you do best.

According to an old business maxim, anything that is measured and watched is improved. The concept of managing by Scorecard has been around for a long time. The idea has been expressed with many different terms. It's been called dashboard, flash report, metrics, pulse report, key performance indicators, Smart Numbers, and so on. Whatever you call it, it contains a handful of numbers that can tell you at a glance how your business is doing.

The unfortunate reality is that most V/I duos don't have a Scorecard. They lack activity-based numbers to review on a regular basis. They might rely on a P&L to tell them the score, but by then it's too late to take meaningful corrective measures. A profit and loss statement is a trailing indicator. Its data comes after the fact, and you can't change the past. With the Scorecard, however, you can change the future.

In order for you to develop and implement an effective Scorecard, here are 7 Truths that both you and your V/I counterpart must buy into. These 7 Truths are followed by the 6 Fundamentals that make a Scorecard effective.

The 7 Scorecard Truths—You Must Believe That . . .

1. What gets measured gets done.
2. Managing metrics saves time.
3. A Scorecard gives you a pulse and the ability to predict.
4. You must inspect what you expect.
5. You *can* have accountability in a culture that is high-trust and healthy.
6. The effort, discipline, and consistency to manage a Scorecard require hard work—but it's worth it.
7. One person must own it.

The 6 Scorecard Fundamentals

These must be in place for a Scorecard to be effective:

1. It will be reviewed with your Leadership Team in the Weekly Level 10 Meeting.
2. It will contain 5–15 numbers.
3. Someone will be accountable for each measurable (who drives it?).
4. Each measurable needs a weekly goal.
5. If the weekly goal is not being hit, you "drop it down" as an issue in your Weekly Level 10 Meeting.
6. You can see 13 weeks of numbers at a glance (helps you see patterns and trends).

If you believe these 7 Truths and faithfully adopt the 6 Fundamentals, you will unleash the power of the Scorecard. Over time, yours will evolve to become an issue-spotting radar that leads you to ask the right questions, at the right time. In turn, you will be positioned to diagnose and take action—much sooner than without a Scorecard.

On the next page is an example Scorecard template:

Who	Measurable	Goal	Weeks													
			1	2	3	4	5	6	7	8	9	10	11	12	13
Sue	New leads	36													
Sue	Initial sales meetings	12													
Sue	Proposals (#)	4													
Sue	Proposals ($)	$300K													
Sue	30-day pipeline	$1.5M													
Sue	Contracts (#)	2													
Sue	Contracts ($)	$150K													
Evan	Projects late	1													
Evan	Projects over budget	1													
Evan	Defects to clients	0													
Evan	Utilization rate	80%													
Carol	Cash balance	$75K													
Carol	A/R > 60 days	< $30K													
Carol	Billing errors	0													

Creating your Scorecard is simple. Use the template above, and brainstorm to come up with the best 5–15 activity-based numbers that you would like to review on a weekly basis. Choose numbers that will give you a pulse on what is going on, as well as the ability to predict the future results of revenue, profit, customer satisfaction, and capacity. Then add the weekly goal you expect for each, and the person who's accountable to hit that number. Please be patient, as it will take one to three months for your Scorecard to evolve into a tool you love.

With your Scorecard created and the other tools in place, along with the 5 Rules you learned in Chapter 5, you now have an infrastructure for your V/I relationship that will go to the root of almost every V/I issue that exists, and then solve it. We ask for your blind faith in implementing these 5 Tools, along with following the 5 Rules, and let the results speak for themselves.

We could have described the 200+ issues that Visionaries and Integrators face in a 500-page book. Instead, to save you a tremendous amount of time and detail, we are taking you right to the root of solving all of those issues— just implementing 5 Tools and 5 Rules.

If you are interested in a true How-To manual for implementing the 5 Tools in your organization, please refer to these additional resources: *Traction* by Gino Wickman, *Get A Grip* by Gino Wickman and Mike Paton, and a variety of other helpful resources available at www.eosworldwide.com.

FURTHER RESOURCES

For a complete set of tools and resources to help you implement the concepts from this book, please visit us at www.rocketfuelnow.com. We invite you to join the community of Visionaries and Integrators and engage in the conversation about how you can get more from your business. We look forward to meeting you there.

Join the community. Find additional tools and resources. Connect with other experts.

www.rocketfuelnow.com

ACKNOWLEDGMENTS

This book would not have been possible without the help and guidance of the following people. We will never be able to thank you enough for your impact on our lives, our work, and this book.

GINO'S FAMILY AND FRIENDS

In my previous books, I have acknowledged all of the people who were a part of the creation of EOS, which were many. With this very focused topic, I'd like to acknowledge the people who contributed to the Visionary/Integrator discovery and made this specific book possible.

Kathy, my amazing wife, for being such a supportive partner. Thank you for appreciating and understanding my entrepreneurial ways. You are so beautiful, real, and creative. I love you with all of my heart.

Alexis and Gino, my two incredible kids. You are the light of my life; you keep me humble and always remind me what life is truly about. Words cannot describe how much I love you, and I couldn't be more proud of the two of you.

Linda Wickman, my mom, for inspiring me with your strength and wisdom, for our talks, and for always making me feel so loved.

Floyd Wickman, my dad and one of the great Visionaries of our time. You are the embodiment of this work. Thank you for being such a great father, teacher, mentor, and confidant. Thanks for giving me the opportunity to be the Integrator to your Visionary; it was the breeding ground for this work.

Sam Cupp, my business mentor. Thank you for teaching me most of what I know about business and for introducing me to the concept of "Visionary." Your unexpected passing was a great loss to the many lives you've touched. I miss you terribly.

Michael Gerber, the original small business guru. Thanks for your groundbreaking work, for being a pioneer, and for mentioning the word "integrate." It provided the spark.

Karen Grooms, the world's greatest assistant. It's been a wild 20 years together. Thanks for holding it all together and making me look good; I know it's not easy. You are one of a kind, and I greatly appreciate you.

Mark C. Winters, my co-author. It has been an absolute pleasure creating this important work together. You took what would have been good and made it truly great.

The EOS Worldwide Leadership Team (Don Tinney, Amber Baird, Lisa Hofmann, Tyler Smith, and Ed Callahan) for running the show and allowing me to stay in creation mode.

My 126 clients, for 15 years of trusting me to help you build great companies and letting me "practice" on you a little bit. This Visionary/Integrator discovery was cemented through our work together.

Glenn Yeffeth of BenBella Books, my publisher. After I was turned down by over 30 publishers on my first book, you took a chance on me and published it. Thanks for your total commitment to my cause and for publishing my last three books with total belief and willingness to "ride the train." It gives me great confidence and freedom to be creative. It has been a true win/win relationship.

MARK'S FAMILY AND FRIENDS

Beth, my beautiful and strong wife. Thanks for giving me the freedom to be me and pursue my entrepreneurial quests. Thanks for believing in me and being my partner throughout the journey—even when it didn't make sense. And thanks for being such a great mother to our three sons. I sure am lucky to be your husband.

Austin, Blake, and Carson, my amazing sons. You have changed me more than you can know. My world has so much meaning because of you. You've humbled me, cracked me up, terrified me, and given me renewed hope. Your pain hurts me more deeply, and your joy lifts me even higher. You make me better. I sure am lucky to be your dad.

Dr. Richard L. Winters, my father. I couldn't have asked for a better role model. Thanks for showing me the path to a life of purpose. Thanks for always believing in me and telling me "there's nothing you can't do if you'll just set your mind to it." It always felt like you really meant that—so I believed you. I sure am lucky to be your son.

Joyce Winters, my mom. Thanks for all the little thoughtful things you did for me. And the hugs—I sure do miss those. I can't imagine a child feeling more love than I did growing up—and yet you always pushed me to be my best. I still see your sweet smile from the last time I held your hand. I miss you. I sure am lucky to be your son.

Richard B. "Rick" Winters and Cindy Winters Gilmore, my older brother and sister. Thanks for loving me so much. You've always looked out for me and challenged me. It's so comforting to know that if I ever need someone, you'll be there. Thanks for setting such a great example. I sure am lucky to be your little brother.

Gino Wickman, my mentor, coauthor, partner, and friend. You have literally changed my life. Because of you I have finally found my true calling, and I'm now able to spend more time on that than anything else. You challenge me to be my best because that's what you expect from yourself. I've learned so much on this project, and I suspect that's just the tip of the iceberg. I sure am lucky to be your friend.

CONTRIBUTORS

Visionary/Integrator contributors: Scott Bade, Richard Baker, Dave Bitel, Stephen Blocki, Nathan Bohannon, David Bristol, Milli Brown, Curtis Burstein, Jorge

Camargo, Darton Case, Del Collins, Matt Coscia, Ellyn Davidson, Joe DeMaria, Paul Dietz, Michael Dresden, Rob Dube, Eric Ersher, Patrick Fehring, John Glover, Scott Goemmel, Doug Hamburger, Tim Haugh, Link Howard, Dan Israel, Jason Kos, Roxanne Laney, Jeff Lau, Leonard Lynskey, Joe Mackey, Keith Meadows, John Nachazel, Florian Oger, Joel Pearlman, Geoff Piceu, Randy Pruitt, Dave Richards, Will Rosellini, Matt Rossetti, Renee Rouleau, Sam Rozenberg, Marc Schechter, Bob Shenefelt, Eugene Sherizen, Richard Simtob, Jared Sloane, Brandon Stallard, Rob Tamblyn, Jason Teshuba, Mike Uckele, Keith Walters, and Rick Webster.

The manuscript readers: Scott Bade, Steven Bailey, Steve Barone, Matt Bartel, Matt Bergstrom, Stephen Blocki, Rene Boer, Mark Bowlin, Paul Boyd, Linda Bryan, Darton Case, Jeff Connelly, Jim Coyle, Matt Curry, Mark D'Andreta, Hamsa Daher, Ellyn Davidson, Len "Zack" DiGrande, John Dini, Michael Dresden, CJ Dube', Rob Dube, Bob Dubois, Patrick Fehring, Teresa Finn, Tom Giftos, Chris Glick, John Glover, Jeff Goodstein, Chelsea Green, Amy Guinan, Clint Hooper, Dan Israel, Donald Janacek, Ron Johnsey, Darin Klemchuk, Dan Kosmalski, Robb LaCasse, Jeff Lau, James Leneschmidt, Leonard Lynskey, Duane Marshall, Eve Mayer, Keith Meadows, Michael Morse, John Nachazel, Andrew Nehra, Mike Nehra, Sean O'Driscoll, Piyush Patel, Cindy Phillips, Geoff Piceu, John Pollock, Dave Richards, Matt Rossetti, Todd Sachse, Jonathan Smith, Brandon Stallard, Shannon Streater, Jason Teshuba, Don Tinney, Michael Visentine, Keith Walters, Floyd Wickman, Jason Williford, Austin

Winters, and Jason Zimmerman. Thank you for all of your precious time and valuable feedback. You are forever a part of this book.

Other contributors: Walt Brown, Mark Abbott, Pavan Muzumdar, Jason Williford, Mike Frommelt, CJ Dube, Mike Paton, Jim Beauchamp, Dan Wallace, Adam Kaplan, Steve Glisky, David Kohl, Gary Walstrom, Rob Fricker, Kevin Suboski, Matthew Carnicelli of Carnicelli Literary Services, John Paine of John Paine Editorial Services, Drew Robinson of Spork Design, Veronica Maddocks, Glenn Yeffeth and the team at BenBella Books—thank you for helping us shape this story to effectively share it with the world.

And to all of our clients: We are so grateful to be blessed with the opportunity you give us each day—to do the work we love, with the people we love. It is our work together with you that has inspired and informed this book. Thank you for being real, caring deeply, and wanting more from your business. And thank you for inviting us to share your journey. This book would not exist without you.

ABOUT THE AUTHORS

Gino Wickman's passion is helping people get what they want from their businesses. To fulfill that passion, Wickman created the Entrepreneurial Operating System® (EOS), a holistic system that, when implemented in an organization, helps leaders run better businesses, get better control, have better life balance, and gain more traction—with the entire organization advancing together as a healthy, functional, and cohesive team. Wickman spends most of his time as an EOS Implementer, working hands-on with the leadership teams of entrepreneurial companies to help them fully implement EOS in their organizations. He is the founder of EOS Worldwide, a growing organization of successful entrepreneurs from a variety of business backgrounds collaborating as certified EOS Implementers to help people throughout the world to experience all the organizational and personal benefits of implementing EOS. He also delivers workshops and keynote addresses.

Mark C. Winters has a passion for helping entrepreneurs get unstuck so they can pursue their freedom. Depending on the unique situation, Mark's talent for introducing just the right combination of perspective and process sparks teams to start moving, move faster, or begin moving in the proper direction with clarity. As a teacher, coach, and facilitator, Mark spends most of his time directly engaged with entrepreneurial leadership teams as a Certified EOS Implementer—helping them implement EOS in their own companies. A seasoned professional with over 25 years of entrepreneurial leadership experience, his companies have ranged from raw startups originally drawn up on a napkin, to multibillion-dollar global enterprises such as Procter & Gamble and British Petroleum. This diverse background enables him to identify and apply patterns of success to virtually any business scenario. Mark is known for pursuing business opportunities related to systems that enable the optimization of human/athletic performance, with a special interest in pattern recognition and scoring methodologies. Outside of his studio, you're likely to find Mark coaching a youth football team on a field somewhere.